I0605741

GREECE

BY CARLA MOONEY

Essential Library
An Imprint of Abdo Publishing
abdobooks.com

ABDOBOOKS.COM
Published by Abdo Publishing, a division of ABDO, PO Box 398166, Minneapolis, Minnesota 55439.

Printed in China.
052025
092025

Cover Photo: Shutterstock Images (ruins, pattern)
Interior Photos: Roman Sigaev/Shutterstock Images, 4–5; Andrew Michael/Education Images/Universal Images Group/Getty Images, 7; Boris Riaposov/Shutterstock Images, 8; Tatjana Baibakova/Shutterstock Images, 10; Shutterstock Images, 11, 12, 16 (globe), 23, 33, 40, 64–65, 77, 81, 82, 87, 92; Sven Hansche/Shutterstock Images, 14–15; Red Line Editorial, 16 (map); Gabriela Insuratelu/Shutterstock Images, 19; iStockphoto, 20; Vaclav Matous/Shutterstock Images, 24–25; Dmitry Laudin/Shutterstock Images, 26; Jordi Jornet/Shutterstock Images, 29; Gonzalo Jara/Shutterstock Images, 30; Richard Garvey-Williams/Alamy, 34; PHAS/Universal Images Group/Getty Images, 36–37; history_docu_photo/Alamy, 38; North Wind Picture Archives/Alamy, 41; Werner Forman/Universal Images Group/Getty Images, 42; DEA/G. Nimatallah/De Agostini/Getty Images, 45; ullstein bild Dtl./Getty Images, 46; Kostas Tsironis/Bloomberg/Getty Images, 50; Martin Beddall/Alamy, 52–53; Hulton Archive/Getty Images, 55; Menelaos Myrillas/SOOC/AFP/Getty Images, 56; Ayhan Mehmet/Anadolu Agency/Getty Images, 58–59; Smith Archive/Alamy, 62; Alan Diaz/Getty Images Sport/Getty Images, 63; Reynold Mainse/Design Pics Editorial/Universal Images Group/Getty Images, 66–67; Milos Bicanski/Getty Images News/Getty Images, 69; Costas Baltas/Anadolu Agency/Getty Images, 70; Tony Papageorge/Shutterstock Images, 73; Nicolas Koutsokostas/NurPhoto/Getty Images, 74; Mateusz Slodkowski/SOPA Images/LightRocket/Getty Images, 78–79; Ville Palonen/Alamy, 85; Peter Phipp/Travelshots.com/Alamy, 88–89; Dima Moroz/Shutterstock Images, 93; Aris Messinis/AFP/Getty Images, 96–97; Viacheslav Lopatin/Shutterstock Images, 98–99; Viktoriia Chorna/Shutterstock Images, 101

Editor: Marley Richmond
Series Designer: Maggie Villaume

Library of Congress Control Number: 2024948581

PUBLISHER'S CATALOGING-IN-PUBLICATION DATA
Names: Mooney, Carla, author.
Title: Greece / by Carla Mooney
Description: Minneapolis, Minnesota: Abdo Publishing, 2026 | Series: Essential library of countries | Includes online resources and index.
Identifiers: ISBN 9781098296971 (lib. bdg.) | ISBN 9798384919490 (ebook)
Subjects: LCSH: Geography--Juvenile literature. | Greece--Juvenile literature. | Europe--Juvenile literature. | Greece--History--Juvenile literature.
Classification: DDC 949.5--dc23

CONTENTS

CHAPTER **ONE**

A TOUR OF GREECE

Amira peeks out her airplane window and studies the sprawling city and blue waters below. It's midmorning when the plane touches down at Athens International Airport, also known as Eleuthérios Venizélos. It is named for one of Greece's prime ministers. The airport is in Spata, Greece, about 17 miles (27 km) east of downtown Athens.[1] Amira grabs her bag and follows her parents and sister out of the bustling airport.

A taxi carries Amira and her family from the airport to a hotel in Athens's city center. Athens is Greece's capital. It sits in the southeast of Greece's mainland. At the hotel, Amira and her family quickly check into their rooms and drop off their bags.

Plaka is the oldest neighborhood in Athens, Greece. Outdoor markets are held in the neighborhood's central square, which is a popular gathering place.

Amira remembers the Greek mythology unit from her social studies class. Her teacher had taught the class several exciting stories about gods, heroes, and legendary creatures from Greek mythology. Amira loved the tales about powerful gods and goddesses who ruled the world from Mount Olympus. Some of her favorites were Zeus, the king of the gods; Artemis, the goddess of the hunt; and Ares, the god of war. Now Amira is excited to start her Greek adventure and see how ancient Greek myths relate to modern Greece and everyday Greek life. With her family, she steps outside to explore Athens.

ELEUTHÉRIOS VENIZÉLOS

Eleuthérios Venizélos was an important politician in modern Greek history. Venizélos was born on the Greek island of Crete in 1864. He served as Greece's prime minister for a combined 13 years between 1910 and 1933.[2] He formed the country's first political party, the Party of Liberals. Many places throughout Greece honor Venizélos by bearing his name.

GREECE'S CAPITAL CITY

Athens is crowded with a mix of residents and tourists. As Amira walks through the streets, she soaks in everything there is to see. Athens is nothing like the Pennsylvania town where she has lived all her life. She notices how past and present are side by side across the city. An old cobblestone street leads to a busy market where vendors sell their goods in stalls. At the same time, sleek shopping centers around the corner serve customers. Amira's father reminds the family of how Athens got its name. The city was named after Athena, the Greek goddess of wisdom. The ancient Greeks believed Athena was the city's protector.

Amira and her family walk into the Plaka neighborhood, where most streets are closed to vehicles. They stroll past shops and buildings decorated with stunning greenery and colorful flowers. Cafés, restaurants, and open-air tavernas also line the street. Tavernas are popular meeting spots for locals and tourists, where social gatherings often last well into the night. Amira can't wait to stop at one and try Greek food later in the day.

ATHENA, GODDESS OF WISDOM

In Greek mythology, Athena is the goddess of wisdom and the patron of Athens. According to myth, Athena was born under unusual circumstances. Her father, the god Zeus, discovered a prophecy that stated his child with the nymph Metis would one day become the lord of heaven. Zeus did not want this to happen, so to prevent it from coming true, he swallowed the pregnant Metis whole. When it was time for Athena's birth, the god Hephaestus used an axe to open Zeus's head. Athena emerged, dressed in full battle armor.

THE ACROPOLIS OF ATHENS

The Plaka neighborhood sits at the base of one of Greece's most impressive sites, the Acropolis. Amira and her family walk uphill toward the entrances of the ancient ruins. Amira learned in social studies class that the Acropolis of Athens is a complex of temples dedicated to Athena. The ancient ruins of these temples sit high on a hilltop overlooking the capital.

The family joins a tour group and listens as the guide explains the history of the Acropolis.

The Erechtheion was built to honor several ancient Greek gods. One of the structure's roofs is supported by six sculpted women instead of traditional columns.

In 447 BCE, Athenian leader Pericles ordered its construction. Four significant monuments were built between 447 and about 400 BCE: the Parthenon, Erechtheion, Propylaea, and Temple of Athena Nike. Talented architects, sculptors, and other artisans continued to add new structures, temples, and monuments to the complex. It became Athens's political and religious center.

The tour group walks across to the Parthenon. This temple sits at the highest point of the Acropolis. Amira stands in front of the impressive ruins and studies the massive white columns that are still standing. She tries to imagine how the temple looked in its prime. The tour guide explains that 46 white marble columns once lined the outer perimeter of the Parthenon. Each column stood 34 feet (10 m) tall and six feet (1.8 m) wide.[3]

The Parthenon was built from 100,000 short tons (90,700 metric tons) of marble.[4]

Brightly painted statues and carved scenes decorated the temple. Today Amira sees that while many of the outer columns are still standing, the marble is damaged in places. Also, many of the temple's original statues, its decorations, and its roof are gone. The structure opens to the sky.

After exploring the Acropolis, Amira and her family walk to a traditional taverna. They choose one with outdoor seating, where locals and tourists engage in lively conversation at the tables around them. The restaurant offers a variety of mezes, or small plates, each day. Amira's family chooses several to share. When the food arrives, Amira decides that her favorite dish is *saganaki*, an appetizer of pan-fried cheese.

FERRY TO THE ISLANDS

After a few days exploring Athens, Amira and her family board a ferry to the Greek island of Mykonos. When they reach the island, they are greeted by its white sand beaches and bright blue waters. A few hours later, the family enjoys a walking tour of the island. Amira inhales the salty scent from the ocean as she and her family stroll past fish and vegetable markets along the island seafront.

Greek mezes often include olives, peppers, cheeses, and seafood to share.

They stop for photos at the Paraportiani Church, a famous example of Cycladic architecture. Its asymmetrical, whitewashed walls have rounded edges and little decoration. Next, Amira and her family reach Alefkandra, an area of the island known as Little Venice. There, old houses rest nearly at the ocean's edge. Near the harbor, windmills face north, overlooking Little Venice and the ocean.

Later on their trip, Amira and her family travel to Santorini, another Greek island. It is also called Thera. Amira's mom reads a pamphlet on the island's history. She learns it was reshaped by an enormous volcanic eruption in about 1600 BCE.

The volcano's eruption released massive amounts of magma from an underground chamber. The empty magma chamber could no longer support the volcano on top of it, and both the chamber and the volcano collapsed. The collapse created a large depression called

Paraportiani Church is made of five smaller churches built together. They were constructed over several hundred years.

Several blue-domed churches dot Santorini's cities. These buildings were painted white and blue to represent the colors on the Greek flag.

a caldera. The ocean submerged the caldera's center. Its rim jutted above the ocean's surface and formed a circular group of islands, including Santorini.

Amira laces up her sneakers for a hike on Santorini's rim of the caldera. The six-mile (10 km) hike follows the path that farmers, sailors, and other island inhabitants have traveled for centuries.[5] The trail takes Amira and her family through several villages with whitewashed buildings, terraced gardens, and churches topped by iconic blue domes scattered throughout the cliffs overlooking the ocean.

WHITEWASHED ISLAND HOUSES

On many of Greece's rocky islands, houses were built with stone. It was more plentiful than wood. Some people painted the dark stones of their homes white to reflect the sun's intense rays and help keep their houses cool. A cholera outbreak in 1938 led Greece's government to order the whitewashing of all homes. Cholera is a bacterial infection of the intestines that spreads easily. The whitewash contained limestone, which is a natural disinfectant that helped sanitize homes. Although Greek people are no longer required to paint their homes white, many still use the traditional white and blue colors.

After the walk, Amira and her family return to their Santorini hotel. At dinner, they discuss their plans for the next day: a snorkeling trip in the clear waters of Santorini's Red Beach. Amira is thrilled to explore more of Greece.

EMBRACING THE PAST AND PRESENT

More than 33 million visitors from around the world travel to Greece every year.[6] Officially named the Hellenic Republic, the small country is located in southeastern Europe. Greece is bordered by three seas: the Aegean, Ionian, and Mediterranean.

Greece's history, monuments, spectacular island scenery, and delicious cuisine make it a beautiful place to live or visit. Known as the birthplace of Western civilization, Greece offers many ancient sites and artifacts that give visitors a unique glimpse into the past. It has miles of incredible coastline and beaches along its mainland and thousands of islands. And for many, a visit to Greece would not be complete without enjoying Greek foods, such as traditional souvlaki, a tasty skewer of meat, and sweet, flaky baklava.

CHAPTER **TWO**

GEOGRAPHY

Greece is in southern Europe, south of Albania, North Macedonia, and Bulgaria. Greece is a relatively small country, with a total area of 50,949 square miles (131,957 sq km).[1] It is a little smaller than the US state of Alabama.

Greece is bordered by three bodies of water. The Ionian Sea lies to the west, while the Mediterranean Sea borders Greece in the south. The Aegean Sea lies to the east and separates Greece from Turkey. Greece also includes about 6,000 islands, but only about 227 of them are inhabited by people.[2]

GREECE'S MAINLAND AND PENINSULAS

Greece can be divided into three main geographical regions: the mainland, the Peloponnese peninsula,

Algae are plantlike organisms that can make bodies of water look green and murky. The Mediterranean is so blue because the sea doesn't have enough food for algae to grow.

MAP OF

GREECE

NORTH MACEDONIA
BULGARIA
ALBANIA
Thessaloniki
Mount Olympus
Aliakmonas River
Northern Pindos National Park
CORFU
Meteora Monasteries
AEGEAN SEA
TURKEY
Temple of Apollo
EUBOEA
Patras
Corinth
Acropolis
Mycenae
Athens
MYKONOS
IONIAN SEA
PELOPONNESE PENINSULA
SANTORINI
Heraklion
CRETE
MEDITERRANEAN SEA
N
W
E
S

KEY:

- Capital
- City
- Point of Interest

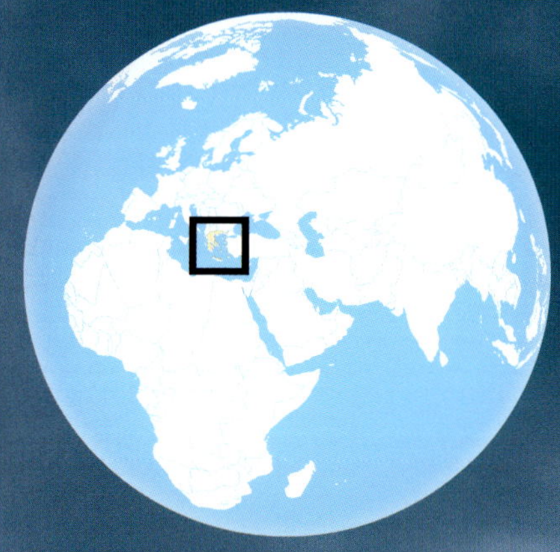

CORINTH CANAL

In 1882 construction began on the Corinth Canal, a waterway across the Isthmus of Corinth. The canal opened in 1893 and connected the Ionian and Aegean Seas. Before the canal, sailors traveling between Europe and Asia had two choices. They could sail the long and dangerous trip around the Peloponnese, or they could stop at Corinth and pull the ships and their cargo over land until they reached the other side. Now, ships traveling between Europe and Asia can sail through the canal to reach their destinations more quickly and safely.

and the islands. Greece's mainland is the country's primary landmass on the Balkan Peninsula. The mainland is home to many of Greece's mountains, lakes, rivers, and forests.

The mainland's coastline is notched with many inlets. An inlet is a narrow strip of water that reaches from the sea into the mainland or between two islands. Greece has so many inlets that most areas of the mainland are fewer than 50 miles (80 km) from the sea.[3]

Greece has numerous peninsulas that extend into the sea. The most significant is the Peloponnese. This peninsula sits in southern Greece. The Isthmus of Corinth connects the mainland to the Peloponnese. An isthmus is a thin strip of land that separates two bodies of water and connects two landmasses. The Isthmus of Corinth separates the Aegean and Ionian Seas.

GREECE'S ISLANDS

Together, Greece's islands form an immense archipelago, or group of islands. The Greek islands make up about one-fifth of the country's total land area.[4] Most of Greece's islands are in the

Aegean Sea, but others are in the Ionian and Mediterranean Seas. The islands vary in size. Greece's smaller islands are also known as islets.

The Greek islands can be divided into six main groups. The Cyclades, Sporades, Dodecanese, Saronic Islands, and North Aegean Islands are all located in the Aegean Sea. Each has a unique character and setting. To the west, the Ionian Islands are scattered along the Greek mainland's western coast in the Ionian Sea. These islands are known for their natural beauty and numerous beaches.

The largest Greek island is Crete, a long, narrow island near the southern point of the archipelago. Crete has a land area of 3,190 square miles (8,260 sq km), making it the fifth-largest island in the Mediterranean Sea.[5] The island has varied landscapes, including caves, valleys, forests, rugged mountains, and deep gorges. Sandy beaches and rocky cliffs line Crete's coasts. Greece's second-largest island is Euboea, which covers 1,411 square miles (3,655 sq km) in the Aegean Sea.[6] Other large Greek islands include Lesbos, Rhodes, and Chios.

MOUNTAINS, CANYONS, AND GORGES

Mountains rise and fall throughout Greece. Approximately 80 percent of the country is mountain terrain, making it the third-most mountainous European country, after Norway and Albania.[7] Most of Greece's mountains are on the mainland, but some are on the islands. Crete is home to several notable mountains and ranges, including the White Mountains, Mount Ida, and the Dikti Mountains. Greece's mountain regions are home to some of Europe's oldest forests, which

WHITE MOUNTAINS MYTHOLOGY

Greece's White Mountains get their name from the mountains' limestone rock and snow-covered peaks. In Greek mythology, the White Mountains in Crete formed after a battle between the Greek gods and a group of giants. The giants challenged the Greek gods but were defeated. The giants' bodies turned into stone, forming the impressive White Mountains. Legend claims many ancient battles and supernatural events occurred in the mountain range. As a result, the mountains' peaks and valleys are said to be haunted by spirits.

provide valuable habitats for plants and animals. As a result, many of these regions are protected as national parks.

One of the largest mountain ranges in Greece is the Pindos. The Pindos range runs through the center of mainland Greece and is known as the nation's backbone. The range stretches from about 100 miles (160 km) south of Greece's border with Albania in the northwest to the Peloponnese in the southeast. The Pindos mountains were formed by volcanic activity more than 65 million years ago.[8] The highest peak in the Pindos is Mount Smólikas at 8,652 feet (2,637 m) high.[9] The range's steep slopes descend into deep canyons.

The Vikos Gorge, one of the deepest canyons in the world, is located in the Pindos range. The Vikos Gorge has dramatic cliffs that rise above a lush valley. The gorge extends 12 miles (20 km) along the southern side of Mount Tymfi in the Pindos range. The gorge's depth ranges from

The Voidomatis River carved Vikos Gorge over millions of years. Several hiking trails traverse the gorge for people to explore.

1,476 to 4,429 feet (450–1,350 m).[10] The gorge is home to many species of plants and animals and is protected as part of Northern Pindos National Park.

Mount Olympus is the tallest mountain in Greece. It is located in northern mainland Greece. On Mount Olympus, 46 peaks rise more than 6,560 feet (2,000 m) high. The tallest of Mount Olympus's peaks is Mytikas, which extends to an elevation of 9,570 feet (2,917 m).[11] Mount Olympus is home to various plants and animals and has been protected as a national park since 1938. This mountain is central in ancient Greek mythology as the home of the Olympian gods. One of the mountain's peaks, Stefani, is known as Zeus's Throne.

LAKES AND RIVERS

Throughout Greece there are many freshwater lakes and saltwater lagoons. Most lakes formed in Greece's interior regions from melting mountain snow. The country's largest natural freshwater lake is Lake Trichonida in west-central Greece. It covers an area of 37 square miles (96 sq km). The lake's deepest point is 187 feet (57 m) deep.[12] Lake Trichonida is fed by water from the nearby Panaitoliko and Arakynthos mountains and underground water sources.

THIRTEEN REGIONS

Greece is divided into 13 geographic and administrative regions called peripheries. Each region has appointed officials that manage the region's development, services, and policies. The Eastern Macedonia and Thrace, Central Macedonia, and Western Macedonia regions reach across the north. Epirus forms the northern border with Albania in the west. Thessaly lies east of Epirus and south of Western Macedonia. Four provinces are located in Greece's southern mainland: Central Greece, Attica, Western Greece, and the Peloponnese. The Greek islands are divided into four regions: the North Aegean, the South Aegean, the Ionian Islands, and Crete.

Greece also has several human-made lakes, including Lake Plastira in Thessaly. People formed these lakes by building dams in rivers, streams, or brooks to stop some water from flowing out. People create artificial lakes to store water to use for various purposes, such as farming or drinking. Greece's human-made lakes also provide an essential habitat for many plants and animals.

Greece's sea lagoons are saltwater lakes near the coastline. One of Greece's most famous sea lagoons is the Sea Lake of Mesolongi. Sediment deposits from two rivers, the Evinos and Acheloos, formed a ridge that separated some water from the

About 60 percent of Greece's coastline is along the mainland. The remaining 40 percent is around its many islands.[15]

sea, forming the lagoon. Swampy wetlands can be found around the lagoon.

Several rivers flow through Greece's cities, towns, and countryside. Rivers have long provided water, food, and habitats for wildlife. Greece's longest river is the Aliakmonas River, also known as the Haliacmon or the Aliákmon River. The river begins in the Grammos Mountains near the Greece–Albania border. It travels about 185 miles (298 km) southeast through valleys and basins in Greece's mainland before flowing into the Aegean Sea at the Gulf of Thérmai.[13]

The Aliakmonas River is an important ecosystem that provides a habitat for several fish species, including European sea bass and brown trout. The river is also essential to agriculture. It provides water for farming and irrigation.

COASTAL REGIONS

Greece's coastline is 8,498 miles (13,676 km) long. The country has the third-longest coastline in Europe.[14] Some areas are made of hard rock. Others consist of coastal cliffs. Some coastal regions feature long, sandy beaches. Others are muddy coasts with fine sediments such as silt and clay.

Greece's long coastline and many islands make the nation vulnerable to rising sea levels due to climate change. As sea levels rise, the existing coast may be covered or eroded. Human-made seawalls and dams can help protect the coastline.

CLIMATE IN GREECE

Greece has a Mediterranean climate. This temperate climate has mild, wet winters and hot, dry summers. The country's climate is affected by its location on the Mediterranean Sea. During summer, temperatures can rise to between 86 and 95 degrees Fahrenheit (30–35°C) on the islands and along Greece's coastal regions. Interior regions are often hotter. Heat waves with temperatures of more than 104 degrees Fahrenheit (40°C) occur regularly each summer in central Greece.[16]

During winter, daytime temperatures range between 50 and 59 degrees Fahrenheit (10–15°C).[17] In mountain regions, higher altitudes lead to colder winter temperatures and snowfall. Snow is rare on the Greek islands, except in the White Mountains on Crete. Northern regions of Greece also typically experience colder winters than southern regions.

Some locations in Greece's mountains are difficult to access after winter snowfalls, such as the Metéora monasteries in the Pindos range.

CHAPTER **THREE**

PLANTS AND ANIMALS

Greece is home to more than 36,000 species of plants, animals, fungi, and other organisms.[1] The nation's Mediterranean habitats provide places for flora and fauna to thrive. Certain protected habitats, such as national parks, are important to protecting the country's biodiversity.

A suitable habitat meets an organism's needs for survival. For animals, a habitat must include food, water, shelter, and mates for reproduction. For plants, a habitat needs to have the right amount of light, air, and water. Plants also require the correct type of soil. Greece's diverse habitats include forests, woodlands, coastal areas, wetlands, grasslands, scrublands, and caves.

The little owl is Greece's national bird. These creatures measure about eight inches (20 cm) in height.

The average olive tree lives for about 500 years, although the oldest-known olive tree has been alive for between 4,000 and 5,000 years.

FORESTS AND FRUIT TREES

Forests and other wooded areas cover nearly one-third of Greece's land.[2] Forests are filled with coniferous trees in the northern regions and higher mountain elevations. Coniferous trees are evergreen trees that bear their seeds in cones. They have needlelike or scalelike leaves. Some common coniferous trees in Greece are firs, black pines, and Aleppo pines.

ATHENA'S GIFT

In Greek mythology, the olive tree was a gift to the Greek people from Athena, the goddess of wisdom. According to legend, Athena and Poseidon, the god of the sea, both claimed Athens. Zeus declared the city would be awarded to the god who gave the most valuable gift to the people of Athens. Poseidon used his mighty trident to crack the rock of the Acropolis and bring forth a saltwater spring. Athena buried a seed in the soil of the Acropolis. The seed grew into a majestic olive tree filled with fruit. The tree was beautiful and useful. It provided timber, food, and oil. Zeus declared Athena the winner, and she became the city's patron goddess.

Deciduous trees, which lose their leaves each fall, commonly grow in forests at lower elevations in Greece. These include poplar, oak, plane, beech, chestnut, and cypress trees. Throughout the forests, various species of shrubs and flowers grow near the base of trees.

One of Greece's most well-known trees is the olive tree. Olive trees are evergreen trees that produce edible fruits called olives. Greece's Mediterranean climate of warm summers, mild winters, and limited rainfall creates a favorable environment for olive trees to thrive. Olive trees grow in groves and gardens across the mainland and the Greek islands. Many are concentrated in the Peloponnese region and the islands of Crete and Lesbos. Several varieties of olive trees produce different variations of fruits. The Koroneiki, Kalamata, Megaritiki, Amfissis, and Throuba are common olive tree species in Greece.

Other fruit trees grow in gardens throughout Greece. Fig trees grow across the nation and can often be spotted along roadsides. Other plentiful fruit trees include orange, lemon, apple, pear, and peach. Almond and walnut trees are common as well.

The carob tree grows across Crete. This tree produces pods that ripen to have a sweet pulp inside. Carob pulp is roasted and ground into a powder that can be used in cooking and baking as a chocolate substitute.

WILDFLOWERS

Approximately 6,000 species of wildflowers bloom across Greece's mainland and islands.[3] Wildflowers grow in areas such as wetlands, coastal plains, and forests. The poppy, with its bright red petals and black center, grows across the country, covering fields and meadows with color in spring. Another common flower, the anemone, produces bright blue, red, or white flowers.

Some flower species are found only in specific areas of the country. For example, the Cretan tulip grows in rocky habitats on Crete. This white-and-pink flower is typically found growing in large colonies. The ironwort blooms with yellow flowers across Greece's mainland and the Peloponnese.

More than 200 species of wild orchids grow throughout Greece.[4] On Mount Olympus, species such as the horned orchid and the monkey orchid can be found. Orchid species such as the horseshoe bee orchid, with its signature silver-colored horseshoe on its large brown petal, are spotted on the Peloponnese.

Many wild orchid varieties also grow on Crete. These include the Cretan bee orchid, which has greenish petals and a distinctive dark, velvety lip with white markings. The ancient Greeks used orchids in medicines to treat digestive problems and improve strength.

ANIMALS IN GREECE

Greece's diverse landscapes provide varied habitats for numerous mammal species. Land mammals in Greece include wild boars, red deer, brown bears, gray wolves, Balkan lynx, and golden jackals. Goats and donkeys are common domesticated land mammals.

The *kri-kri*, also known as the Cretan ibex, lives on Crete. The kri-kri has a light brown coat and two horns on its head. It is nimble on rocky

Orchis simia **got its common name, the monkey orchid, because people say the curly lobes of its petals resemble the limbs of monkeys.**

Striped dolphins are commonly spotted in the Mediterranean Sea. They often swim in deep waters rather than shallow areas near coasts.

terrain, easily climbing steep cliffs and leaping across distances up to 26 feet (8 m).[5] Although the kri-kri once lived across the Aegean region, today it is found only on Crete and a few nearby islands. The kri-kri was designated an endangered species in 1960 when its population dropped to about 200. The species was threatened because of habitat destruction and hunting. Today, hunting kri-kri is strictly regulated, and the population has grown to about 2,000.[6]

Sea mammals such as dolphins and whales swim along the Greek coastline. The dolphin is Greece's national animal. These marine mammals appear in Greek mythology and culture.

Four dolphin species swim in the waters around Greece: the common dolphin, bottlenose dolphin, Risso's dolphin, and striped dolphin. Whale species include the blue whale, sperm whale, fin whale, Cuvier's beaked whale, and humpback whale.

The Mediterranean monk seal is endangered and has a population of about 600 worldwide.[7] Half of the population lives in the seas around Greece. These seals live near sea caves, rocky shores, and deserted beaches on land.

Monk seals dive as deep as 620 feet (190 m) underwater for food.[8] Diving deep allows the seals to find food on the ocean floor and avoid predators such as sharks swimming near the surface. When they dive, their nostrils close to prevent water from entering. Their whiskers spread and help them sense the water around them.

Salmon, tuna, bream, swordfish, anchovies, cod, octopuses, eels, sea bass, and squid also swim through the waters in and around Greece. Loggerhead sea turtles swim in the seas and come ashore to lay their eggs. Greece's freshwater lakes and rivers are home to fish such as trout, minnows, shad, loaches, catfish, and lampreys.

Three amphibian species are found only in Greece. One such species, the Karpathos water frog, lives on the Greek island of Karpathos. This frog can be found near a single river system at the island's northern end. It is primarily aquatic and lives in freshwater lakes and slow-moving streams. This species is critically endangered and faces threats from habitat loss due to human activity. Other amphibians found only in Greece are the Karpathos salamander, which lives on Karpathos, and the Cretan water frog, found on Crete.

Numerous reptile species live across Greece's mainland, peninsulas, and islands, including snakes, lizards, geckos, tortoises, and turtles. Several of the country's snake species are venomous. One dangerous species is the European adder, although its venom is not lethal to humans.

The smallest bird in Greece is the coal tit. The tiny bird weighs about 0.35 ounces (9.9 g).[11]

The nose-horned viper is one of Europe's most dangerous snakes. It is a large snake with long fangs and deadly venom. It can grow to between 33.5 and 37.4 inches (85–95 cm) long from nose to tail.[9] The viper is frequently found in dry and rocky areas, open woodlands, and sand dunes. It can also be found where humans live, especially near piles of rubble and stone walls.

More than 400 bird species are found in Greece.[10] Many migratory species stop in the country for a few weeks as they fly north to south and back again. Common birds include warblers, larks, tits, sparrows, and gulls. Some birds of prey fly across Greek skies, including the golden eagle, white-tailed eagle, peregrine falcon, and Eurasian scops owl. The little owl is Greece's national bird. Known as the owl of Athena, this owl is a symbol of wisdom and knowledge.

Dragonflies and spiders are common in Greece's forests and wetlands. Butterflies such as the two-tailed Pasha, the clouded yellow, and the southern white admiral flutter among fields and wildflowers. Cicadas, also known as *tzitzikas* in Greek, buzz from trees throughout summer. The male cicada sings using a membrane between its chest and abdomen called a tymbal. The song attracts females and deters predators such as birds.

NATIONAL PARKS AND CONSERVATION

Greece has multiple national parks, each of which plays a role in preserving the nation's landscapes, habitats, plants, and animals. The largest national park is Northern Pindos National Park in northwestern Greece. The national park's protected lands cover more than 770 square miles (2,000 sq km), including rivers, forests, mountains, and lakes.[12] Many native fish, foxes, otters, bears, and other animals live in the park's habitats. The deep Vikos Gorge and Mount Smólikas, Greece's second-highest peak, are also in the park.[13]

Across Greece, scientists and conservationists are working together to protect threatened species. Greece is home to many endemic species. An endemic species is found only in a particular place. Some endemic species are found only in a tiny area, such as a specific island, lake, or mountain. These species are particularly vulnerable to habitat loss, climate change, invasive species, natural disasters, and other factors that might change their surroundings.

LOGGERHEAD SEA TURTLES

Greece is home to several nesting beaches for the loggerhead sea turtle. Female turtles return to the nesting beach where they hatched years earlier to lay their eggs. Each turtle builds two to three nests during a single nesting period. In each nest, a single female lays up to 120 eggs.[14] The temperature of the sand helps determine the sex of the hatchlings. Warmer sands produce more females, while more males hatch from cooler sands. The eggs remain in the sandy nest for about two months. Once the eggs hatch, the hatchlings crawl through the sand to the water.

The Greek rock lizard is endemic to the nation. It has distinctive blue-green dots on its sides.

Approximately 22 percent of plant species in Greece are endemic. The country also has more than 4,000 endemic animals, most of which are insects. Greece's national parks, universities, and other organizations have partnered to help preserve vulnerable species. For example, researchers at the University of Athens have stored seeds from more than 400 rare plant species in the school's seed bank.[15] If needed, the seeds can be used to reintroduce a species that has gone extinct.

Several aquatic animal species are endemic to lakes in the Prespa region of northern Greece. To preserve the region's ecosystems, a conservation organization called the Society for the Protection of Prespa organized a project to remove overgrown reeds from the lakes' shallow edges. Overgrown plants interfered with endemic fish species' breeding habits.

By keeping the edges clear, environmentalists allowed the endemic fish population to grow as breeding increased. In turn, these actions helped support local populations of pelicans and herons. These threatened bird species feed on the endemic fish. More food allowed the birds to thrive.

FOREST FIRES

In recent decades, forest fires have destroyed huge swaths of Greek forests. Fires in 2023 were some of the most destructive in recent Greek history. In that year, fires destroyed more than 540 square miles (1,400 sq km) of forests across Greece. Hundreds of structures were also destroyed. More than 20 people died. One fire in Evros near the Turkish border lasted more than 15 days and burned more than 360 square miles (930 sq km) alone.[16]

CHAPTER **FOUR**

HISTORY

Greece has a long history that stretches back thousands of years, covering ancient civilizations, mighty empires, and modern communities. Some of the earliest known settlements in Greece were built between 11,000 and 3000 BCE. Historians believe that the earliest humans in the area arrived from the east. They established settlements, used stone tools, and performed basic farming tasks.

Historians have found evidence that Greek civilizations grew larger and more advanced between 3500 and 3000 BCE. Villages grew, and social hierarchies emerged. The people fished, farmed, created clay pottery, and embarked on sea voyages. The favorable weather conditions in Greece and these advanced settlements likely attracted immigrants and traders from nearby lands. Settlers developed metalworking

Historians have found works of art that date back to ancient Greek civilizations. Bull leaping was a historical activity depicted in one artwork.

The Agora was the political and cultural center of Athens, and its ruins show historians what the city-state may have looked like in ancient times.

skills and practiced a form of religion. As the settlements advanced and grew, people began trading goods with other civilizations.

One of the great early civilizations in Greece was the Minoans on the island of Crete. The Minoans thrived between approximately 2600 and 1500 BCE. They were known for art, trade, and constructing majestic palaces such as Knossos and Phaestos. Another great society, the Mycenaean civilization, rose to power in about 1700 BCE across most of mainland Greece and several islands.

Led by a king and a group of elites, the Mycenaeans were known as skilled craftspeople and engineers. They built palaces protected by fortified walls across Greece, the largest of which was the palace of Mycenae.

ANCIENT GREECE

After the fall of the Mycenaeans in about 1100 BCE, Greece entered a period of little growth or progress for several hundred years. By 800 BCE, numerous independent city-states had emerged. A city-state was known as a *polis*. Each polis had its own government, culture, and traditions. They shared a belief in the Greek gods.

Greece is home to 18 United Nations Educational, Scientific and Cultural Organization (UNESCO) World Heritage sites.[2]

The largest polis was Athens. Athens was unique in that it based its social hierarchy solely on wealth instead of a person's aristocratic status or heritage. Another important city-state was Sparta. Sparta was the first Greek city-state to organize a government assembly that represented all of Sparta's citizens in its political system. More than 150 smaller colonies were also established across Greece and its islands.[1]

In the 500s BCE, the Persian Empire threatened Greece's towns and colonies. The Persian Empire was a powerful civilization located in what is now Iran, Egypt, Turkey, Afghanistan, and Pakistan. The city-states of Athens and Sparta, along with other Greek towns, united to defeat the Persians in several battles.

Athens became the region's dominant power between 500 and 300 BCE. This time, mostly in the 400s BCE, was known as the golden age of Athens. The city prospered with peace and cultural advancement under the leadership of famed general and statesman Pericles.

At this time, Athens developed the first known system of democracy in the world. All male citizens, regardless of social status or wealth, had equal political rights. They had the right to vote, speak, and run for political office. The Athenian democracy was a direct democracy, meaning that citizens made the decisions that governed Athens. They also worked in the institutions that governed the city-state, sharing responsibility for running Athens.

Athens's increasing power and wealth threatened many of Greece's city-states, including Sparta. Sparta wanted more power and control for itself. Spartans were warriors; most men received a military education before joining Spartan forces to defend and expand the polis's land and power. Eventually the rivalry between Athens and Sparta led to the Peloponnesian War (431–404 BCE).

The war gradually enveloped most of Greece's smaller towns as they allied with Athens or Sparta. After years of war, the Spartans eventually

ATHENS'S FIRST CITIZEN

One of ancient Greece's most famous statesmen was Pericles. Pericles was a general and politician during Athens's golden age. On the battlefield, Pericles led Athens's forces during the Peloponnesian War. He was a strong supporter of the arts and literature, which allowed Athens to become a cultural and educational hub. Pericles also started an expansive building program across Athens, including the Acropolis. For his work, Pericles is known as Athens's first citizen.

defeated Athens. However, the victory had a cost, and Greece was weakened as a whole.

After the Peloponnesian War, a kingdom in northern Greece called Macedonia emerged as a new Greek power. The Macedonians, led by King Philip II, defeated Athens and the polis of Thebes in 338 BCE and united towns across Greece. After King Philip's death in 336 BCE, his son Alexander the Great rose to power.

Alexander the Great led the Macedonian Empire to become one of the largest empires in world history. With thousands of Greek soldiers, Alexander invaded and conquered the Persian Empire, including Egypt, Mesopotamia, parts of India, and Asia Minor, an area in southwestern Asia where modern-day Turkey is located. Alexander's forces spread Greek culture and ideas to every land they conquered.

In each place, Greek ideas influenced art, science, and philosophy. After Alexander died in

Athenian forces were defeated in the Siege of Syracuse, a decisive battle in the Peloponnesian War.

MINI **BIO**

ALEXANDER THE GREAT

Alexander the Great was a Macedonian king and one of history's greatest military commanders. Born in Pella, Macedonia, to King Philip II and Queen Olympias in 356 BCE, he was educated by the philosopher Aristotle. Aristotle instilled in him a love for learning and a fascination with the world.

At age 20, Alexander ascended the throne after his father's assassination. Over the next decade, Alexander led military campaigns of conquest. He overthrew the Persian Empire and expanded his empire.

Alexander's genius on the battlefield won him both loyalty and numerous victories, despite often facing armies that outsized his own. He sought to unify the East and West by merging Greek and Persian cultures and founding cities, such as Alexandria in Egypt, which became centers of learning and culture.

Alexander died in 323 BCE at the age of 32 from unknown causes. His empire was split into four parts and given to his generals. Despite his early death, Alexander's legacy lived on, spreading Greek influence and culture and inspiring many future leaders.

Many statues and busts depict Alexander the Great. Some that survive today are reproductions of carvings originally made in the 200s or 300s BCE.

323 BCE, the Macedonian Empire broke apart into separate kingdoms. This event marked the end of ancient Greece.

CHANGING RULERS

Across the Mediterranean Sea, the Roman Empire was expanding its power in Italy. The Greeks had aligned with the Empire of Carthage in modern-day Tunisia to battle the Romans. The two empires endured years of fighting until the Romans prevailed in about 197 BCE. Greece became part of the Roman Empire. The Romans adopted Latin and Greek as the empire's official languages. The Romans also welcomed aspects of Greek culture into their own. Cities such as Athens, Corinth, Alexandria, and Thessaloniki thrived with years of peace and security.

In the first century CE, a new religion called Christianity spread across the Roman Empire. In 324 CE, the Roman emperor Constantine moved the empire's capital from Rome to Byzantium in what is now Turkey. He renamed the city Constantinople. In 364 CE, the Roman Empire split into the Western Roman Empire and the Eastern Roman Empire, better known as the Byzantine Empire.

Greece was part of the Byzantine Empire for nearly 1,000 years. As part of the Byzantine Empire, the Greek people enjoyed a period of prosperity and trade. However, several wars weakened the empire and left it vulnerable. By the 1100s, the Byzantine Empire was in decline.

In 1453 the Byzantine Empire fell when the Ottomans invaded and conquered Constantinople, which the Ottomans renamed Istanbul. The Ottoman Empire originated from Turkish tribes in Asia. The Ottomans ruled Greece for nearly 400 years.

The Ottoman Empire was an Islamic state. Although the Ottomans gave non-Muslim communities some autonomy to rule themselves, these communities also faced challenges. For example, the Ottomans imposed additional taxes on non-Muslims. They also conscripted young men into the military. Many Greek families moved to places such as Russia, Italy, and Austria to escape Ottoman rule. Still, Greek culture persisted despite these challenges.

WAR OF GREEK INDEPENDENCE

After nearly 400 years of Ottoman rule, the Greek people wanted independence. In 1821 several revolts against the Turkish occupiers broke out in the Aegean Islands and the Peloponnese. Within one year, the rebels controlled the Peloponnese, and in 1822 they declared Greece's independence.

Fighting continued for several more years despite the Greek declaration of independence. However, the war tipped in Greece's favor when the Greeks won the support of Russia, Britain, and France in 1826. These countries, known as the Great Powers, asked the Ottoman leader, Mahmud II, to withdraw from Greece. When the Turks refused, the Great Powers sent naval ships to help Greece in 1827. Their fleet attacked and destroyed the Egyptian ships that were helping the Turks.

Although the naval defeat weakened the Turks, the war continued. The war did not end until the Greeks and Turks reached a settlement in 1830. The Treaty of Edirne created an independent Greek state. Ioannis Kapodistrias was elected the first head of state of the new Greek republic. However, Kapodistrias was assassinated in 1831. At that time, Prince Otto from Bavaria in what is now Germany was named the king of the Kingdom of Greece.

MODERN GREECE

The Kingdom of Greece was smaller than the nation is today. It encompassed the Peloponnese, Sterea, the Cyclades Islands, and the Saronic Islands. Throughout the 1800s, Greece attempted to expand its territory to include regions where Greek people lived.

In 1912 the Balkan Wars (1912–1913) erupted when Greece, Serbia, Bulgaria, and Montenegro declared war on the Ottoman Empire. The first war resulted in the Ottoman Empire losing most of its land in Europe. Serbia, Greece, and Romania disagreed with Bulgaria about how to divide the Ottoman conquests, which led to a second conflict. After the Balkan Wars, Greece added Macedonia, Epirus, Crete, West Thrace, and the Aegean Islands to its territory.

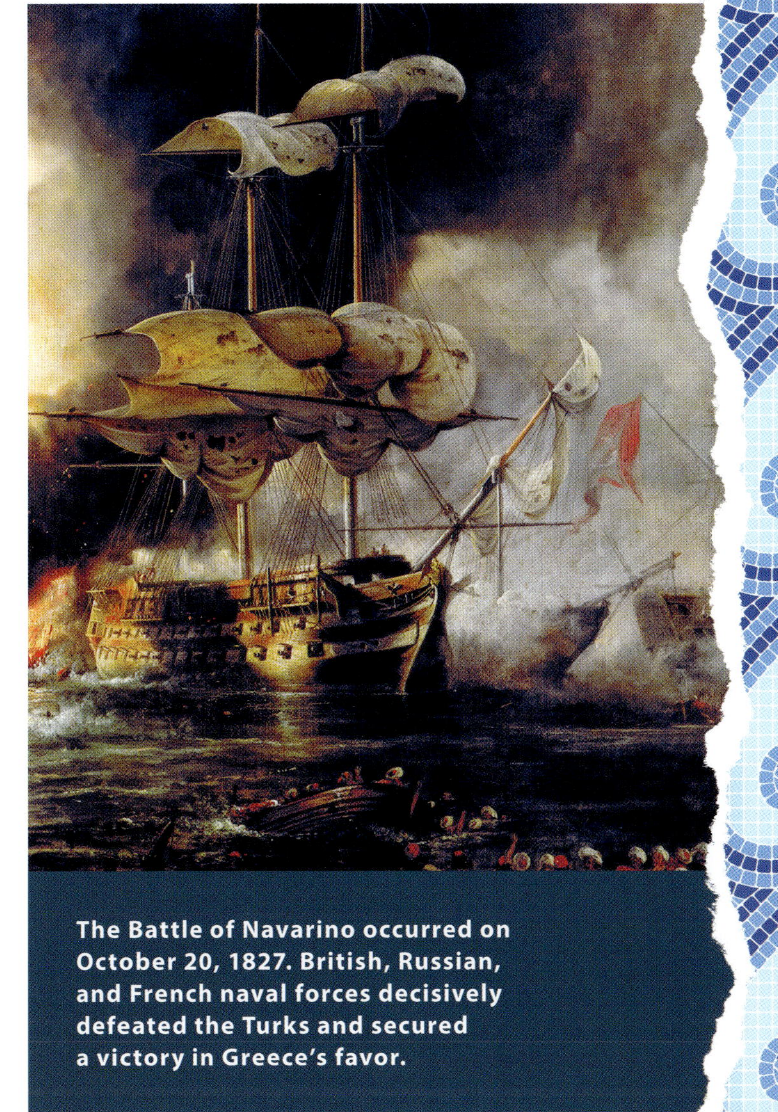

The Battle of Navarino occurred on October 20, 1827. British, Russian, and French naval forces decisively defeated the Turks and secured a victory in Greece's favor.

German military aircraft flew over Athens in 1941 during the German occupation of Greece.

In 1919 Greece attempted to expand into Asia Minor, where many Greeks lived. This expansion led to the Greco-Turkish War (1919–1922). Greece was unprepared for war against the Turks. The nation was ultimately unsuccessful in expanding its territory.

BATTLE OF CRETE

In 1941 the German Army invaded and occupied Greece's mainland. In May the Germans turned their attention to Crete. They launched a parachute and glider attack on the island. Crete's citizens and Allied forces from the United Kingdom, Australia, and New Zealand bravely fought the Germans. However, Crete fell after eight days, and the Allied forces retreated.[3] After the Battle of Crete, the local population continued resistance efforts. They used whatever weapons they could find to sabotage and attack the Germans. The Cretan resistance efforts continued until the end of the war in 1945.

In 1939 World War II (1939–1945) broke out in Europe. Germany, under the authoritarian leadership of Adolf Hitler, invaded Poland. Poland's allies quickly declared war. The war expanded across Europe and later into the Pacific.

On one side of the conflict, Germany, Italy, and Japan were known as the Axis powers. These nations were led by extreme and nationalist governments that sought to expand their territory and spread their ideals. The Allies, led by the United Kingdom, the Soviet Union, and later the United States, fought against the Axis powers.

At first, Greece remained neutral in the war. In 1940 the nation's government refused Italy's demand to occupy Greek territories. In response, Italian forces unsuccessfully attempted to invade. But Axis troops still sought the strategic advantage of occupying Greece. By April 1941, Greece fell to German forces.

Germany occupied the nation until 1944. During this time, several communist groups in Greece joined together as the National Liberation Front. The National Liberation Front fought against the nation's occupiers. The monarchy that had ruled the nation before the war opposed this communist group. Violence often broke out between the two sides, even under German occupation.

By September 1944, the Axis was losing the war. The Germans slowly withdrew from Greece. Several anti-communist groups then joined to fight the National Liberation Front. Meanwhile, Greek and British forces finally forced complete German withdrawal from Greece in October.

In May 1945, German forces surrendered, officially ending the war in Europe. The global conflict ended in September of that year with the surrender of Japan. However, the tension between anti-communist and communist groups that had risen during Greece's occupation remained high.

A violent civil war between communist and anti-communist forces broke out in Greece in 1946. Greek communists attempted to take control of the country. At first the communists were able to control parts of northern Greece. However, the United Kingdom and the United States supported the anti-communist forces.

These nations supplied military equipment and funding to the Greek army, led by the king, helping the army defeat the communist rebels by 1949. An estimated 50,000 people died in the civil war, and more than 500,000 citizens were displaced from their homes.[4] The war left the country divided and economically weakened.

In 1967 a military junta seized control of Greece and ended its monarchy. In the following years, opposition to the junta's military rule caused increasing unrest. By 1974, the junta's military rule fell apart, and Greece became a democracy. In 1975 a new constitution established Greece as a parliamentary republic.

DEBT CRISIS AND RECOVERY

Greece joined the European Economic Community, later the European Union (EU), in 1981. This helped stabilize its economy. During the late 1900s, Greece's government had engaged in wasteful and excessive overspending. To pay its bills, Greece took loans from other governments and private investors. This practice caused Greece's national debt levels to skyrocket.

In 2007 and 2008, a global financial crisis caused banks worldwide to struggle. Across Europe and in the United States, governments were forced to send money to banks that had taken on too much debt and were at risk of collapsing. The Greek government had many loans and was unable to pay the growing interest on its debt. The country's years of government overspending and high debt levels had become unsustainable. The nation's economy was close to collapse.

The International Monetary Fund (IMF) and the EU agreed to bail out Greece from defaulting on its debt. Between 2010 and 2018, the IMF and the EU provided Greece with more than $330 billion in bailout funds. In exchange, Greece agreed to

GLOBAL FINANCIAL CRISIS

The global financial crisis of 2007 and 2008 was the worst economic disaster since 1929's stock market crash. A flaw in the US housing market caused banks across the nation to take on debt through loans that customers could not pay back. Soon the banks had too much debt to continue functioning, and many banks collapsed. Because the world's banking system is interconnected, trouble in US markets quickly spread overseas to Greece and other countries. The world's major economies, including Greece's, entered into a period of economic decline called a recession.

Greeks flooded the streets in 2010 to protest austerity measures implemented to curb the national debt crisis.

implement austerity measures, which included significant government spending cuts and tax increases for citizens. The unpopular austerity measures also included the layoffs of approximately 25,000 public servants, wage and pension cuts, and additional budget cuts.[5] Greece has since worked to recover and stabilize its economy.

In 2020 the COVID-19 pandemic spread worldwide. Like many countries, Greece implemented restrictions and lockdowns during much of 2020 and into 2021. These measures helped prevent the spread of the virus that causes COVID-19. The pandemic struck a major blow to Greece's tourism industry as travel was significantly restricted. However, the country emerged successfully from the early years of the pandemic, and tourism surged above pre-pandemic levels after restrictions were lifted.

CHAPTER **FIVE**

PEOPLE AND CULTURE

Approximately 10.5 million people live in Greece. The median age of the Greek people is 46.5, meaning that half of all Greek people are older than that and half are younger.[1] This makes Greece one of Europe's older populations. The nation's population is slowly declining, and it has a low birth rate compared with the rest of Europe.

Nine out of ten people in Greece are of Greek heritage. The other main ethnic groups in Greece include Albanians, Romani, Aromanians, and Macedonians. Albanians are the largest minority ethnic group in Greece, making up about 4.4 percent of the population.[2] Many Albanians migrated to Greece in the 1990s when the Albanian communist

Cultural events across Greece celebrate the nation's history and diversity. The popular Epidaurus Festival is held in an ancient theater.

government collapsed. They came to Greece looking for work and to make a better life for themselves.

The Romani people, also known as Roma, are an ethnic group originally from northern India. The Roma traditionally travel from place to place and are spread throughout Greece and other European countries. The Roma typically speak a form of the Romani language, which is closely related to modern northern Indian languages.

Greece is in the lower half of European countries in terms of population density. There were an average of 202 people per square mile (78 per sq km) in 2024.[3] This means that in general, the country is more rural than many others in Europe.

About 81 percent of Greece's population is concentrated in urban areas. The largest concentration of people is found in and around the capital city of Athens on Greece's southeastern coast, where approximately 3.15 million people live.[4] Other large cities in Greece include Thessaloniki, Patras, and Heraklion.

GREEK PHILOSOPHERS

Greek philosophers studied ideas about life, knowledge, and the natural world. Well-known Greek philosophers included Socrates, Plato, and Aristotle. Socrates lived in Athens in the 400s BCE and used questions to challenge people's assumptions and beliefs. A student of Socrates, Plato opened one of the earliest universities in Athens in the 380s BCE. Plato's Academy brought people together to study philosophy, law, and mathematics. Aristotle was one of Plato's students and studied many subjects, including philosophy, science, politics, and ethics. Aristotle is known for developing a formal system for reasoning and logic. The ideas of the Greek philosophers have shaped Western ideas and governments for thousands of years. Their work is still being studied worldwide.

LANGUAGE

Greek is the official language of Greece and is spoken by most of the country's residents. Modern Greek directly evolved from the ancient Greek language. Today, Greek is used in the country's official documents, economy, and daily life.

Throughout Greece, several regional dialects of the Greek language are spoken. For example, the Cretan dialect is spoken on the island of Crete. The Zaconian dialect can be heard in the Arcadia region.

The Greek alphabet differs from the Latin alphabet used for English and many other European languages. The Greek alphabet consists of 24 letters. Several letters are the same in the Greek and Latin alphabets, such as *A*, *B*, and *K*. Other Greek letters are not used in the Latin alphabet, such as gamma (Γ), theta (Θ), and xi (Ξ).

The Romani are a disadvantaged group who have faced discrimination since the Ottoman Empire. Today many Romani people live in poverty.

In 2020, after decades of opposition, Athens opened its first official mosque in nearly 200 years. Tzistarakis Mosque provides a place of worship for the city's growing Muslim population.

Other languages are also spoken in various regions across Greece. Many Greek people speak English, which is often used as a common language to communicate with tourists and visitors. Turkish is often spoken in the Thrace region, which borders Turkey. In the Epirus region, Albanian is spoken by Albanian immigrants and people of Albanian descent. Near the border with North Macedonia, some Slavic people speak Macedonian.

RELIGION

Greek Orthodox is the largest religion in Greece, with about 88 percent of the population identifying as Greek Orthodox. The Greek Orthodox Church, also known as the Church of Greece, is a division of Christianity. It is one of several branches within the Eastern Orthodox Church.

In 1054 the Eastern Orthodox Church split from the Roman Catholic Church to become a separate Christian denomination. A small percentage of people in Greece practice non-Christian religions, including Islam at nearly 6 percent. Approximately 4 percent of Greeks report that they do not practice any religion.[5]

The Greek Orthodox Church has an important role in Greek culture. Many Greeks celebrate traditional Orthodox sacraments such as baptism, chrismation, confession, and Holy Communion. Sacraments for marriage, ordination, and anointing of the sick are also very important traditions. In Greece, the Greek Orthodox religion and national identity are linked. More than three-quarters of the Greek public say that being Orthodox is an important part of being a true Greek.[6]

HOLIDAYS

Easter is the most sacred holiday in Greece. It celebrates the resurrection of Jesus Christ, who Christians believe is the son of God. Eastern Orthodox Easter is always on a Sunday in April or May. The week before Easter, Holy Week, is filled with traditions, church services, candlelit processions, and a midnight mass on Holy Saturday. At midnight, the church bells ring to announce the resurrection of Jesus. Families exchange eggs that are dyed red to represent the blood of Jesus and renewal. They eat lamb soup called *magiritsa* together. On Easter Sunday, many people celebrate with family and friends by eating roast lamb and other foods.

Oxi Day is celebrated on October 28 to remember the day Prime Minister Ioannis Metaxas refused to allow Italian forces to occupy Greece during World War II. In Greek, *oxi* is the word for "no." People commemorate this holiday with parades and festive celebrations.

Greek Independence Day is celebrated on March 25. It marks the day the Greek people revolted against the Ottoman occupiers. It was the beginning of the War of Greek Independence (1821–1832). Each year, people in Athens hold a special bell-ringing ceremony to remember the beginning of Greece's battle for independence.

ART AND ARCHITECTURE

Greece is widely recognized for significant contributions to art and architecture. Ancient Greek artists created statues of gods, athletes, and everyday people. They aimed to make their sculptures look realistic, as if they were alive. Some famous statues, such as *Discobolus*, the discus thrower, feature detailed muscles and a sense of movement. One of the most famous Greek sculptures is *Venus de Milo*, also known

Every year, Athens celebrates Greek Independence Day with a parade.

as the Aphrodite of Milos. This marble statue was carved by the artist Alexandros of Antioch in about 150 BCE.

Modern Greek artists such as Nikiforos Lytras, Yannis Tsarouchis, and Chryssa have been recognized worldwide for their talent. The painter Lytras is considered by many to be the father of modern Greek painting. He embraced realism in his paintings of everyday Greek life in the 1800s. Tsarouchis was a painter known for using his work to explore Greek identity and mythology. Chryssa worked in a variety of media and was known for being a pioneer in light art and sculpture. She often used materials such as neon, steel, aluminum, and glass in her work.

Ancient Greek architects designed and built some of the most iconic buildings of the ancient world. Greek architecture is known for its simplicity, harmony, and proportion. These qualities are found in temples, theaters, stadiums, and other structures throughout Greece. Modern Greek architects still use many of the same principles. For example, classic Greek columns are frequently used in the design of public buildings, museums, banks, and even private homes.

GREEK COLUMNS

The column is a well-known part of Greek architecture. The ancient Greeks used three primary column styles. Doric columns were the simplest and thickest style. They had shallow vertical grooves; a simple capital at the top, which attaches the column to the structure it supports; and no base. The Doric column was wider at the bottom and narrower at the top. Ionic columns had a thin, grooved shaft that rose from a base to a capital decorated with scrolls. Corinthian columns were the most decorative style. The grooved shafts rose from a base to a highly decorated capital with scrolls and leaves.

LITERATURE AND MYTHOLOGY

The ancient Greek people used myths to help explain the world around them. Many myths are fictional, such as stories of the hero Heracles. He was said to be a demigod, the son of Zeus and a mortal woman. Stories chronicle Heracles's adventures, battles, and quests. Other myths are inspired by actual events, such as the Trojan War. Initially myths were passed down orally from generation to generation. Eventually they were written down.

The epic poems the *Iliad* and the *Odyssey* by Homer are some of the most well-known stories of Greek mythology. Homer lived sometime between 900 and 700 BCE. The *Iliad* occurs during the Trojan War and tells the story of Achilles, a warrior who was the son of a Greek king and a sea goddess. The *Odyssey* tells the story of the Greek king Odysseus as he travels home from the Trojan War. In each epic poem, the characters encounter gods, monsters, and challenges throughout their journeys.

Several modern Greek authors and poets have made lasting contributions to Greek literary culture. Níkos Kazantzákis was a prolific Greek writer who published several important literary works during the 1900s. His most famous novels include *Zorba the Greek*, *Freedom or Death*, and *The Last Temptation of Christ*. Kazantzákis was nominated several times for the Nobel Prize for Literature but never won. Poet George Seferis became the first Greek to win the Nobel Prize for Literature in 1963.

The *Iliad* has 15,693 lines, while the *Odyssey* is slightly shorter at 12,110 lines.[7]

MINI **BIO**

GEORGE SEFERIS

George Seferis was a Greek poet and diplomat. He is considered one of the most significant figures in modern Greek literature. Born in Smyrna, Greece, in 1900, Seferis and his family moved to Athens in 1914. He studied law at the University of Paris, which laid the foundation for his long diplomatic career.

Seferis returned to Athens in 1925 and began working as a diplomat for the Royal Greek Ministry of Foreign Affairs. Throughout his career, he held diplomatic posts in the United Kingdom, Albania, Turkey, Lebanon, Syria, Jordan, and Iraq. He was the Royal Greek Ambassador to the United Kingdom between 1957 and 1961 before he retired.

Seferis's world travels gave him plenty of time and perspective for his writing. While living overseas, he wrote many of his 12 books of poetry, essays, and fiction. His poetry combines personal experiences, historical events, and Greek identity. His work often explores themes of exile, alienation, and memory. Seferis's significant works include *Strophi* and *Mithistórima*, a collection of short poems inspired by Homer's *Odyssey*.

George Seferis was born with the name Georgios Seferiades.

GREEK FOOD

Greek food is famous for its fresh flavors and ingredients. A staple in Greek cooking is olive oil made from olives grown across the country. In many dishes, olive oil is used liberally, giving Greek food its rich taste. Fresh produce such as tomatoes, cucumbers, onions, and peppers are common and often mixed into Greek salads with feta cheese and olives.

One popular Greek dish is moussaka. This is a layered casserole with eggplant, ground lamb, spices, and a creamy béchamel sauce made with butter, flour, and milk. Another popular food is souvlaki, which is marinated meat, such as pork, lamb, or chicken, served on skewers.

Gyros are a traditional Greek food that can be eaten on the go. A gyro is made with pork, lamb, or chicken alongside tomatoes, onions, and tzatziki, all wrapped in pita bread. Tzatziki is a creamy sauce made from yogurt, cucumber, garlic, and herbs. It is often served as a dip or dressing on gyros and other dishes.

Greek meals often include seafood caught along Greece's long coastline. Grilled fish with

THE SOUNDS OF YANNI

Yiannis Chryssomallis, better known as Yanni, is one of Greece's most famous musicians. He was born in 1954. Yanni is a composer, pianist, and music producer. He is known for creating music with electronic synthesizers, full orchestras, and instruments from cultures worldwide. Yanni's musical style is a unique blend of jazz, classical, rock, and world music. Sixteen of his albums have reached the top of the *Billboard* Top New Age album chart. Yanni has sold more than 25 million albums worldwide and written soundtracks for movies and television.[8]

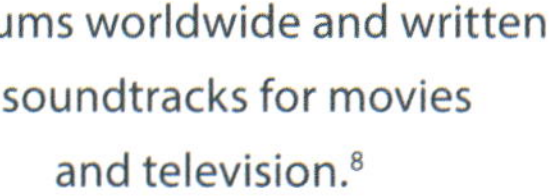

Spanakopita is a popular Greek dish made with flaky pastry, feta cheese, and spinach.

lemon and oil is a commonly prepared dish. Baklava is a Greek dessert made with layers of flaky pastry, honey, and nuts. Greek food is meant to be enjoyed slowly, often with friends and family, making it not just a meal but a celebration of community and tradition.

SPORTS AND RECREATION

Sports have been popular in Greece since ancient times. Greece is the birthplace of the Olympics, with the first Olympic Games being held in 776 BCE. Competitive running, jumping, and gymnastics can be traced back to the ancient games. Athens was also the first city to host the modern Olympic Games in 1896.

Today Greece's national sport is soccer, which Greeks call football. Basketball is another sport that has increased in popularity in recent years. In 2013, Greek professional basketball player Giannis Antetokounmpo joined the Milwaukee Bucks, a team in the National Basketball Association (NBA) in the United States. He helped the team win a championship in 2021.

CHAPTER **SIX**

POLITICS

The modern Greek government was established in 1975. The nation is a parliamentary republic. In this system of government, citizens elect representatives to a governing body, called a parliament, to make laws and decisions on their behalf.

Greece's constitution set up the three main branches of the country's national government: the legislative, executive, and judicial branches. Each branch has designated powers and responsibilities. These are balanced so each branch is equal. Certain individual and social rights are also granted by the constitution, such as citizens' right to vote.

EXECUTIVE BRANCH

Greece's executive branch of government includes its president and prime minister. The president of

Greece's Parliament is housed in what used to be the royal palace. The building's architectural features represent historic Athenian styles.

A constitutional amendment must be proposed by at least 50 lawmakers. Greece has amended its constitution four times, in 1986, 2001, 2008, and 2019.[1]

Greece is a primarily ceremonial position. The Greek parliament elects the president to a five-year term for a maximum of two terms. As the country's head of state, the president represents Greece at international events. The president ratifies and publishes laws passed by Parliament and works with the prime minister to appoint government officials. The president is also responsible for calling Parliament into session and declaring that a federal election will be held.

The prime minister is Greece's head of government. Typically the prime minister is the leader of the political party with the most seats in Parliament. The prime minister appoints ministers to head different departments of the government, which are called ministries. These include the Ministry of Finance, the Ministry of Foreign Affairs, the Ministry of Health, and others.

The prime minister oversees the implementation of the country's laws and the operation of public agencies to benefit the Greek people. The prime minister may also propose laws to Parliament. Greece's prime minister represents the nation internationally, meeting with leaders of other countries and international organizations.

THE HELLENIC PARLIAMENT

The Hellenic Parliament is the legislative branch of Greece's government. Greece's parliament is unicameral, which means it has a single house. Parliament consists of 300 members, called

Katerina Sakellaropoulou became Greece's first female president in 2020.

members of Parliament (MPs), who are directly elected by the people. Greek citizens who are at least 25 years old can run for a seat in Parliament.

Parliament's primary responsibility is to draft and pass laws. MPs can propose new legislation, called bills, along with amendments and additions to other bills. Ministers in the executive branch can also propose new legislation, called law proposals. Each new bill or law proposal is discussed and debated by Parliament. A majority of Parliament must approve a bill for it to become law. Once a bill has been approved, it is sent to the president, who publishes all passed legislation within one month.

Greece held a snap election in June 2023 after no majority government was formed in the May election. Elected MPs were sworn in on July 3, 2023.

Parliament is also responsible for overseeing the Greek government's actions. It can question executive branch officials and hold them accountable for their decisions and policies. Parliament also approves government budgets.

PARLIAMENTARY ELECTIONS

Nationally, Greece holds elections for MPs every four years. However, if the prime minister and their ministers lose support in Parliament, the president can dissolve the current government and call for a snap election to elect a new parliament. Greek citizens must be at least 17 years old to vote in national elections.

Greece's parliamentary elections are based on a proportional representation system. Political parties must win at least 3 percent of votes to win any of the 300 seats in Parliament. Each party that reaches the 3 percent minimum is awarded its share of 285 seats based on the percentage of votes it received. For the remaining 15 seats, state deputies elected by each party fill 12, and three are reserved for candidates elected by Greek citizens voting from overseas.

If no party wins a majority of seats, two or more parties can work together to form a coalition government. This means multiple parties join together into one temporary party that will have a majority. If parties cannot agree to form a coalition government, then a repeat or snap election is held to ensure one party has majority. In this election, the party that wins the most votes receives a bonus of 20 seats if it secures more than 25 percent of the vote. The party can win additional bonus seats, up to 50 if they reach 40 percent of the vote. This system was designed to increase the chances of one party winning a majority of parliamentary seats, which encourages a stable and productive government.

JUDICIARY

The third branch of Greece's government is the judiciary. The judicial branch consists of courts that have the power to interpret laws. The courts resolve disputes between citizens or between citizens and the government. The president appoints judges at the recommendation of ministers. Only lawyers can be appointed, and they must have practiced law for at least two years. They must also pass an exam and complete one year of advanced legal training. Judges are appointed for life after completing a two-year probationary period.

Greece's judicial system has three types of courts: civil, criminal, and administrative. Administrative cases typically include those that involve money claims, social security claims, claims against the government, and challenges to government actions. Civil and criminal courts hear civil cases such as those involving disputes over property, contracts, and family law.

Criminal cases involve crimes against an individual or the state, such as theft, assault, and murder. Civil and criminal courts belong to the same jurisdiction, meaning that judges assigned to this jurisdiction can hear either type of case. Judges assigned to the administrative jurisdiction can hear only administrative cases.

Within each jurisdiction, there are three levels of courts. Cases typically start in the lower courts. Above the lower courts, 13 Courts of Appeals across Greece hear cases that challenge

The Areios Pagos is named after an ancient Greek court founded between 1500 and 1300 BCE.

decisions made by lower courts. The Areios Pagos is the Supreme Civil and Criminal Court of Greece. Fifty-six judges in total make up the Areios Pagos, and they sit in panels of five to hear cases. Supreme Court cases review the legal correctness of lower courts' decisions. The Council of State is the highest court for the administrative jurisdiction. This court determines whether laws follow the Greek constitution.

LOCAL GOVERNMENT

Greece has several levels of local government. The country has seven decentralized administrations, which are divided into 13 total administrative regions made of more than 300 municipalities.[2] Each decentralized administration is led by a secretary-general appointed

In the early to mid-2020s, the Panhellenic Socialist Movement party worked to regain the popularity it had lost in 2010 following the Greek economic crisis.

by the central government. The secretaries-general are responsible for ensuring that national government policies are being implemented at the regional level. They also act as liaisons between regional governments and the national government.

Each of the 13 administrative regions is led by an elected governor and a regional council, all of whom serve five-year terms. The regional government oversees local concerns such as

HEALTH CARE IN GREECE

Greece's health-care system combines public and private services, providing limited universal coverage funded mainly through taxes. All Greek citizens have access to public health care. However, the public health system faces challenges such as staff shortages and long wait times. Many people turn to private care for faster access, even though these services are not covered by public insurance.

education, public transportation, and local economies. Municipalities are the lowest level of local government. An elected mayor and a municipal council oversee each municipality's public safety, urban planning, community events, and general welfare.

POLITICAL PARTIES

Greece has a multiparty political system. Several political parties compete for seats in Parliament during national elections. The main parties in Greece are New Democracy (Nea Dimokratia, or NK), Syriza (also called the Coalition of the Radical Left), and Panhellenic Socialist Movement (PASOK).

The New Democracy party is a center-right party that supports conservative values, including the ideas of a free-market economy, private ownership of businesses, and individual freedoms within a system of law and order. It also supports Greece's membership in the European Union and use of the euro currency. One of its priorities is economic stability for Greece. In 2023 New Democracy won a majority in Parliament with 158 of 300 seats.[3]

The Syriza party is a left-wing political party that supports progressive values and ideals. It promotes issues of social justice and environmental protection. The party also works to reduce poverty and social inequality. In 2023 Syriza won 48 of 300 seats in Parliament.[4]

PASOK is a political party that supports socialist ideals. It also champions policies that encourage public or state ownership of land, factories, and businesses. It advocates for policies that promote social justice and equal opportunities. In 2023 PASOK won 32 seats in Parliament.[5]

HELLENIC COURT OF AUDIT

The Hellenic Court of Audit was founded in 1833. This special court reviews government spending to ensure public funds are used appropriately. The court reviews government accounts, performs audits on public organizations, and investigates financial mismanagement. It ensures that public-sector transactions are legal. The court provides a report of its work to Parliament. The court's work deters corruption and helps safeguard public funds.

MILITARY

Greece's military is the Hellenic Armed Forces, which consists of an army, navy, and air force. The Greek Ministry of National Defense oversees the Hellenic Armed Forces. Because Greece is a member of the United Nations, the EU, and the North Atlantic Treaty Organization (NATO), the Hellenic Armed Forces participates in peacekeeping missions around the world in addition to protecting Greece.

All male citizens of Greece between the ages of 19 and 45 are required to serve in the Hellenic Armed Forces for at least 12 months.[6] Those who try to evade mandatory military service can be fined or face other penalties. Women can volunteer for military service, but they are not required to serve. A Greek citizen living permanently outside of Greece can postpone their required military service. Once they reach age 45, they can be permanently excused from military service.

POLITICAL SYMBOLS

The Greek flag was designed in 1821, but it was not officially adopted to represent the nation until 1978. The design includes nine horizontal stripes, alternating blue and white, and a white cross in the upper left corner. The cross represents the importance of the Greek Orthodox faith in the nation.

The Greek national anthem, "Hymn to Liberty," was written as a poem in 1823. It honors the soldiers who fought in the War of Greek Independence. The poem was set to music in the following decades and adopted as the national anthem in 1865.

NORTH ATLANTIC TREATY ORGANIZATION

The North Atlantic Treaty Organization (NATO) is a political and military alliance formed in 1949 following World War II. There are 32 members of NATO, including Greece, which joined in 1952.[7] NATO's primary goals are to promote democratic values, achieve peaceful resolutions to disputes, and ensure the safety and security of member countries. Every day, military and civilian experts gather at NATO's headquarters in Brussels, Belgium, to share ideas and information.

CHAPTER **SEVEN**

ECONOMICS

Greece's official currency was once the Greek drachma. In 2001, Greece began using the euro. This made Greece a member of the eurozone, a group of countries in the EU that use the euro as their official currency. After two months of dual circulation of the Greek drachma and euro, the euro replaced the Greek drachma in February 2002.

The European Central Bank issues the euro. This is the second-most-traded currency on the world's foreign exchange markets, after the US dollar.[1] The euro is also a major global reserve currency. Global reserve currencies are held in large amounts by central banks or other monetary authorities as part of their reserves.

Greece has many shops where people can buy souvenirs. Most of these stores accept only euros, so people traveling from abroad should ensure they have the correct currency.

Global reserve currencies can be used in international transactions and investments, and they are often considered safe and stable.

MAJOR INDUSTRIES

In 2023 Greece had an estimated gross domestic product (GDP) of $375.8 billion. GDP is the total amount of income generated from the sale of goods and services in a country over a certain period of time. It measures the economic strength of a nation. When measured by GDP, Greece's national economy ranked fifty-fifth largest in the world in 2020.[2]

Travel and tourism are an integral part of Greece's economy. In 2023 income from travel and tourism made more than 19 percent of the nation's GDP.[3] Greece ranked third highest among EU countries in this metric.[4] Only Croatia and Portugal relied more on travel and tourism as part of their economies that year.

Tourists enjoy the country's architecture, archaeology, arts, culture, scenic landscapes, famous cuisine, and historic sites. Millions of tourists visit Greece each year to see sights such as the Acropolis in Athens, the Temple of Apollo on the slopes of Mount Parnassus, the Delphi ruins, the Metéora monasteries, the Theater of Epidaurus,

EUROPEAN UNION

In 1981 Greece joined the European Union (EU). The EU is a political and economic alliance of European countries. It was formed to improve and strengthen European economic and political cooperation after World War II. The EU requires its members to follow specific laws about trade, security, immigration, and environmental protection.

Delphi is a UNESCO World Heritage site. A museum and cultural center inform tourists about the area's rich history and archaeological discoveries.

and the ancient city of Mycenae. Vacationers travel to Greece's beautiful beaches on the islands of Santorini, Crete, Mykonos, and Corfu. The tourism industry employs many people, including those who work in restaurants, hotels, shops, and transportation. In 2023 travel and tourism provided more than 800,000 jobs.[5] That year Greece was the ninth-most-visited country in the world.[6]

Shipping is also an important part of Greece's economy. Today Greece has one of the largest merchant fleets in the world. Greek shipowners control 21 percent of the global merchant fleet as measured by deadweight tonnage. That is the total weight a ship can safely carry. In 2021 shipping contributed nearly 7 percent of Greece's GDP.[7]

Every year more than 38.5 million short tons (35 million metric tons) of cargo move through the Port of Piraeus.

Agriculture provided almost 4 percent of the GDP in 2023, a smaller but still important piece of the Greek economy.[8] Major crops and products include olives, olive oil, wine, tobacco, fruits, and vegetables. Organic farming has become increasingly popular as part of sustainable development plans. However, most of Greece's landscape cannot be used for agriculture because of existing forests or poor soil.

The industry sector in Greece includes manufacturing, construction, mining, electricity, water, and gas. Industry contributed approximately 15.7 percent of the GDP in 2023.[9] Some common products manufactured in Greece are textiles, processed foods, and cement.

IMPORTS AND EXPORTS

Greece lacks natural energy resources such as oil, which makes it dependent on foreign energy. As a result, Greece's main imports are fuels, including crude petroleum and petroleum gas. In 2023 Greece imported $18.6 billion in crude petroleum and petroleum gas, which was nearly 21 percent of total imports.[10] Other major imports included cars, pharmaceutical products, machinery, equipment, plastics, iron, and steel. Greece's top import partners are Germany, China, Italy, Iraq, and the Netherlands.

Some of the crude petroleum that Greece imports is processed, refined, and then exported. In 2023 Greece exported $14.6 billion of refined petroleum oils and oils from bituminous materials. These include asphalt and tar. Together, Greece's refined oil products accounted for 26 percent of the country's total exports.[11]

Medicines and medical supplies were the second-largest export. They contributed 5.2 percent of Greece's exports in 2023, totaling $2.9 billion. Exports of aluminum produced $1.2 billion, or 2.3 percent of total exports.[12] Other major exports include olive oil, cheese, fish, and electrical energy. Greece's main export partners are Italy, Bulgaria, Germany, Cyprus, and the United States.

Overall, Greece imports more goods than it exports. In 2023 Greece exported $55.1 billion in goods, while it imported $88.6 billion.[13] Because it imports more goods than it exports, Greece has a negative trade balance, also called a trade deficit. Trade deficits are not always bad for a nation's economy. However, over time they can cause a country to go into debt if the nation borrows money to cover the cost of its imports.

NATURAL RESOURCES

Greece has a variety of natural resources. These include mineral deposits such as iron ore, lead, zinc, nickel, magnesite, and salt. Lignite, a type of soft brown coal, is primarily found in Western Macedonia and the Peloponnese. Bauxite, an ore used to make aluminum, is abundant throughout the country.

In addition to minerals, Greece has significant reserves of marble. Greek marble comes in various colors, including white, off-white, gray, green, black, and red. Greek marble is known for its high quality and is used worldwide in construction and art projects. Greece has more than 200 active marble quarries, with the majority found in Eastern, Central, and Western Macedonia.[14]

ENERGY SOURCES

Greece relies on four primary sources to supply its energy: coal, oil, natural gas, and renewables. Oil is the most widely used energy source, providing 54 percent of Greece's energy in 2023. Natural gas provided about 21 percent of the country's energy supply, while coal provided 6 percent. Solar and wind renewables provided about 11 percent of the energy supply.[15] Other renewables, including hydropower, supplied the country's remaining energy needs.

Greece's labor force consisted of an estimated 4.65 million people in 2023.[17]

In 2023 Greece's energy imports comprised 90.3 percent of the country's total energy supply.[16] This heavy reliance on imported energy sources leaves Greece vulnerable to supply disruptions due to natural disasters, wars, and other events. Recognizing its reliance on energy imports, Greece has made a significant effort to invest in renewable energy sources.

Greece's long coastlines and many islands provide a favorable environment in which to generate wind and solar power. In 2023 Greece's production of wind, solar, and hydroelectric energy reached a record high. Electricity generated by renewable sources and hydroelectric plants accounted for 57 percent of Greece's total electricity generation in 2023, although this remained a smaller percentage of the country's total energy used.[18]

TRANSPORTATION

People and goods move throughout Greece via roads, railways, ship ports, and airports. Several ports and harbors around the country

Some marble quarries produce stone known by name, such as Thassos Snow White marble.

handle goods and passengers traveling to and from Greece and its islands. The Port of Piraeus is the largest port in Greece and the second largest in the Mediterranean area. It sits on the Saronikos Gulf on the southeast of Greece's mainland. From Piraeus, ships sail to the Black Sea, Indian Ocean, and Atlantic Ocean. Other significant ports include the Port of Thessaloniki, Port of Volos, Port of Milos Island, and Port of Heraklion.

ATHENS METRO NETWORK

In Athens, the Metro network is a subway system that connects Athens's city center with nearby suburbs. The Metro runs more than 50 miles (80 km) across three lines. More than 100 trains and 66 stations serve approximately 1.3 million passengers daily.[20] When the Metro was constructed, workers found approximately 50,000 ancient artifacts, including ceramic vessels, toys, and the remains of ancient bridges.[21] Several metro stations now display some of these artifacts.

Eighty-one airports across Greece welcome travelers and goods. On Greece's mainland, Athens International Airport is Greece's largest airport. More than 28.2 million travelers passed through it in 2023.[19] In northern Greece, the Airport of Thessaloniki is the country's second-biggest airport. Other well-traveled airports include those of Heraklion, Santorini, and Mykonos.

Cars, buses, trucks, and motorcycles travel over the thousands of miles of highways and paved roads across Greece. The roads connect rural and urban populations. Railways also connect cities across the mainland, although the nation's bus system is known to be more reliable and convenient than its railways. Ferries carry people and goods from the mainland to the Greek islands and from island to island.

RECESSION RECOVERY

Greece entered a severe recession for a decade after the global financial crisis and Greek debt crisis in the late 2000s and early 2010s. However, the country has slowly made progress in restoring its economy. In 2022 Greece paid off the IMF for its bailout loans two years early.[22] The Greek banking system has recovered, and the country no longer needs additional bailout funds to finance the government. Between 2020 and 2023, the nation's GDP grew steadily and remained on track to continue to rise faster than the average of other eurozone countries.

However, for the Greek people, signs of the economic recovery are slow. Many people still have not recovered financially from the economic crisis. Unemployment was still higher than 10 percent, the second highest in the EU, in 2024. The average monthly salary in 2024 was 20 percent lower than the average salary 15 years earlier.[23]

INTERNATIONAL MONETARY FUND

The International Monetary Fund (IMF) is a global organization dedicated to the growth and prosperity of its 191 member countries, including Greece. It was created in 1944 after the Great Depression of the 1930s. The IMF promotes global economic policies that achieve financial stability and cooperation. Its experts can provide economic advice to member countries. The IMF also provides loans and financial aid to members when necessary.

CHAPTER **EIGHT**

GREECE TODAY

In Greece, daily life revolves around the family. Most Greek families live in a single household with immediate family members. Extended family members often live nearby and visit frequently. Sometimes adult children will bring aging parents into their homes to provide care, as many Greek families have an unfavorable view of nursing homes and care facilities.

In Greek families, children are taught to respect elders and the wisdom that comes with age. Younger people often ask elderly family members to give input on major decisions. Many Greek children live with their parents into adulthood, sometimes even as newlywed couples.

Families and friends often socialize outdoors in Greece's warm weather.

Grandparents have an important role in the lives of their grandchildren, helping raise the children and watching them frequently. Traditionally many Greek children are named after one of their grandparents. Godparents are also an important part of family life in Greece. When a child is born, many parents select a godmother and godfather who pledge to take responsibility for the child if anything happens to the parents. Godparents are usually close friends or family members.

FAMILY BUSINESS

For Greeks, the importance of the family extends to business. In 2020 approximately 80 percent of business owners in Greece described their businesses as family run.[1] Many of these businesses are small and employ fewer than ten people. Many operate in retail, services, and construction industries. Most family business owners plan to keep their businesses in the family and pass them to the next generation. Passing businesses to the next generation does not mean the owners are finished, however. Many plan to keep working in their family businesses even after retirement.

TRADITIONS AND CELEBRATIONS

In Greek families, traditions and celebrations are important. Milestone events are a reason to have large family celebrations. One of the biggest celebrations is a Greek wedding. It is customary that when one person is invited to a wedding, their entire immediate family is also invited. Some weddings can have more than 1,000 guests. At a typical Greek wedding, the religious ceremony is followed by a large party with live music and Greek dishes. Dancing is enjoyed by all, including the youngest and oldest guests.

For Greek babies born in 2024, life expectancy is about 82 years.[2]

Baptism is another important Greek tradition. In the Greek Orthodox Church, a child's baptism celebrates the day the child becomes a Christian. Baptism typically occurs between the ages of 18 months and three years. Godparents traditionally pay for the items the priest uses during the baptism ceremony, including a white towel, candles, and new clothes for the child.

During baptism, the child is submerged in the baptismal water three times. The priest makes a cross with holy water on the child's forehead. The celebration begins after the child is dried and dressed in new clothes. The party typically includes live music, food, and dancing. Guests pin a *martyrika*, a small cross and ribbon, to their clothes and receive *koufeta*, traditional candy-coated almonds, at the baptism celebration.

Across Greece, many people celebrate their name days. Many Greek children are named after a religious saint or martyr. Throughout the year, certain days are dedicated to different saints and martyrs. Greek people celebrate on the day dedicated to their namesake saint or martyr. These celebrations are similar to birthday parties, and people invite family and friends to join them for the festivities.

GREEK HOSPITALITY

Beyond the family, socializing with friends is a central part of daily life in Greece. Socializing often takes place in local cafés and restaurants. Gathering with friends for coffee is a daily practice for

Olive oil is used in Orthodox ceremonies as a symbol of religious protection.

Greeks of all ages. Younger Greeks often frequent modern cafés for coffee and pastries, while older Greeks might be seen at a *kafeneio*, a traditional café that has been around for many years. Every village and town has several kafeneios, which are traditionally local meeting places for older men. People may spend the morning relaxing at kafeneios, reading newspapers, playing cards or other games, talking about current events and politics, eating, and drinking.

Many Greeks welcome friends and family to their homes and pride themselves on their hospitality. No invitation is needed to drop by a friend's or family member's home. Visitors are welcomed inside and offered food and drink regardless of the day or time. Many hosts even expect their visitors to bring friends to join them. Some Greek people keep extra food and drink on hand just in case an unexpected visitor arrives.

Recreational activities are another way to socialize in Greece. Mountain sports, such as hiking, climbing, and skiing, are popular throughout the mountainous country, as is hunting. Team sports such as field hockey, baseball, and cricket are played across the nation.

GODS IN DISGUISE

Greek hospitality may be traced back to an ancient belief that a visitor could be one of the Greek gods or goddesses in disguise. Everyone was expected to welcome guests and offer food, drink, and a place to stay, no matter their wealth, title, or social status. According to legend, Zeus punished those who did not offer hospitality. Showing hospitality would help a person gain favor with Zeus and the other Greek gods.

EDUCATION

Education is highly valued in Greek culture. The government runs schools under the oversight of the Hellenic Ministry of National Education and Religious Affairs. The education system has several levels. Students attend primary school, two levels of secondary school, and can optionally attend higher education institutions. Public education is free at all levels, including higher education. All children ages four to 15 are required to attend school.

Children begin their education at age four. They attend kindergarten before entering primary school at age six. In primary school, students learn reading, writing, math, English, and environmental studies. Academic classes are typically held in the morning and early afternoon. After the academic classes are done, many primary schools offer additional art, music, and physical education classes. Students graduate from primary school at about age 12.

After primary school, students enter the first level of secondary school, called *gymnasio*. In gymnasio, students aged 12 to 15 study math, science, geography, history, and modern and ancient Greek language. They also have classes in religious studies, art, and physical education. Students continue taking foreign language classes, including both English and another European language.

After gymnasio, most students attend an optional second level of secondary school called *lykeio*. Students take a combination of general education and advanced placement courses in humanities, science and medical studies, finance, and computer science. Some students enroll in vocational schools instead, where they study general education courses and learn workplace skills.

Students may then choose to continue to higher education. Higher education institutions include universities and technical institutions, where students can pursue bachelor's, master's, or doctoral degrees. University entrance is highly competitive, and students must take nationwide Panhellenic exams as part of their applications. Many students spend months preparing for these exams.

GREEK DIASPORA

Over the centuries, many Greek people have traveled from Greece to live abroad in countries worldwide. According to estimates from Greece's government, more than five million people of Greek heritage live outside of Greece today. These people are referred to as the Greek diaspora. They live in approximately 140 countries worldwide.[4] Many are concentrated in the United States, Germany, Australia, Canada, the United Kingdom, and Albania. In many areas, diaspora members embrace the traditions and culture of Greece, keeping their connection to the country strong.

CHALLENGES

Greece has faced several challenges in recent years, including human rights concerns. Greece's location along the Mediterranean coast has made it a gateway to Europe for people fleeing violence and conflict in the Middle East, Africa, and Asia. Between 2014 and 2024, more than 2.5 million people entered Greece to escape conflict and crises in their home countries. Many pass through the nation and make their way to another country, but more than 550,000 refugees and asylum seekers remained in Greece during those years.[3]

Greece has faced accusations of cruel treatment of migrants and asylum seekers, including claims that the nation forced migrants to return to Turkish seas even in dangerous conditions.

Many migrants face danger when traveling to Greece on often-flimsy vessels in turbulent waters.

In June 2023, a ship carrying approximately 750 people, including many migrants, sank near the coast of Pylos. Only 104 people survived.[5] A number of survivors reported that the Greek coast guard had towed the ship with a rope, which caused it to tip and capsize. The Greek coast guard denied that it tried to tow the ship.

Greek journalists report that the government has limited their ability to freely report on issues through restrictive regulations and engaging in surveillance. In 2022 a scandal exploded in Greece. The illegal spy software Predator was found monitoring journalists, politicians, and other public figures through their cell phones.

After a two-year investigation, Greece's Supreme Court Prosecution Office declined to find a government ministry or agency responsible for the spyware. Many people were critical of the decision. They accused the government of attempting to cover up the spying scandal.

Youth unemployment is another challenge facing Greece. In 2024 youth unemployment reached 20 percent, higher than the EU average of 14.5 percent.[6] The youth unemployment rate includes members of the country's labor force aged 15 to 24. High unemployment adds financial strain on the country because unemployed people receive monthly payments from the government. A lack of job opportunities and limited vocational training have contributed to youth unemployment.

A PROMISING FUTURE

Once the home of ancient civilizations, Greece has transformed into a modern nation. Yet it still cherishes its rich history and culture. The past and present blend together to create a uniquely Greek experience.

Today Greece is home to countless artistic, historical, and cultural treasures that draw visitors from around the world. Some visitors sail from island to island, soaking in the Mediterranean sun and tasting the latest Greek cuisine. Others explore ancient sites to learn about the nation's long history. As Greece balances its past and present, the future looks bright for the country and its people.

People come to Greece to walk in the steps of the ancients and marvel at the modern nation's beauty.

ESSENTIAL **FACTS**

OFFICIAL NAME: HELLENIC REPUBLIC

GEOGRAPHY

Area: 50,949 square miles (131,957 sq km)

Highest Elevation: Mount Olympus at 9,570 feet (2,917 m)

Lowest Elevation: Mediterranean Sea at 0 feet (0 m)

PEOPLE

Population: 10.5 million (2024 est.)

Most Populous City: Athens (3.15 million)

Ethnic Groups: Greek, Albanian, Romani, Aromanian, Macedonian, other

Religions: Greek Orthodox, Islam, other, none, unspecified

GOVERNMENT

Type of Government: Parliamentary republic

Capital: Athens

Head of State: President

Head of Government: Prime minister

Legislature: Unicameral Hellenic parliament

ECONOMY

Currency: Euro

Major Industries: Tourism, food and tobacco processing, textiles, chemicals, metal products, mining, petroleum

Natural Resources: Lignite, petroleum, iron ore, bauxite, lead, zinc, nickel, magnesite, marble, salt

NATIONAL SYMBOLS

National Anthem: "Hymn to Liberty"

National Motto: *Eleftheria i Thanatos* ("Freedom or Death")

National Bird: Little owl

GLOSSARY

audit

An official inspection of a group's or business's financial and organizational accounts, usually by an independent party.

communist

Having to do with a system in which the government controls the economy and owns all property.

conscript

To force people to enlist in the military.

decentralized

Spread out across several locations rather than contained in one central hub.

immigrant

A person who moves to a new country permanently.

junta

A group that controls a government after a revolution.

jurisdiction

A certain area within which a group has authority to make a legal decision or take legal action.

migrant
A person who moves from one place to another, often to find work or better living conditions.

patron
A person or figure chosen as the guardian, protector, or supporter of a place.

public servant
A person who is appointed or elected to work for a government.

public-sector
Controlled by the government.

sacrament
A religious rite or ceremony in the Christian church.

sediment
Tiny fragments of rock and other particles that settle and form a layer.

vocational
Related to a skill or trade that can be pursued as a career.

ADDITIONAL **RESOURCES**

SELECTED BIBLIOGRAPHY

"Greece's Debt Crisis Timeline." *Council on Foreign Relations*, n.d., cfr.org. Accessed 13 Nov. 2024.

Kouras, Bill. "The Practical and Historical Reasons behind the Blue and White Colors of Greek Island Houses." *Greek City Times*, 26 Nov. 2023, greekcitytimes.com. Accessed 5 Nov. 2024.

Steves, Rick. *Rick Steves' Greece: Athens & the Peloponnese*. Avalon, 2023.

FURTHER READINGS

Averbuck, Alexis, et al. *Experience Greece*. Lonely Planet, 2023.

DuBois, Jill, et al. *Greece*. Cavendish Square, 2023.

Pearson, Anne. *Ancient Greece*. DK, 2023.

ONLINE RESOURCES

To learn more about Greece, please visit **abdobooklinks.com** or scan this QR code. These links are routinely monitored and updated to provide the most current information available.

MORE INFORMATION

For more information on this subject, contact or visit the following organizations:

Acropolis Museum

Dionysiou Areopagitou 15
Athens 117 42
theacropolismuseum.gr/en

The Acropolis Museum is an archaeological museum. People can explore findings from the Acropolis's archaeological site at the museum or on its website.

National Archaeological Museum

44, 28th of October (Patission) St.
Athens 106 82
namuseum.gr/en

The National Archaeological Museum is Greece's largest museum. It holds more than 11,000 artifacts gathered from every place where Greek civilization flourished.

National Hellenic Museum

333 S. Halsted St.
Chicago, IL 60661
nationalhellenicmuseum.org

The National Hellenic Museum in Chicago, Illinois, has a mission to share Greek history, culture, and art. It honors the contributions of Greek immigrants and Greek Americans to the United States.

SOURCE **NOTES**

CHAPTER 1. A TOUR OF GREECE

1. "Getting There in Athens." *Frommer's*, n.d., frommers.com. Accessed 17 Jan. 2025.
2. "Eleftherios Venizelos." *Greeka*, n.d., greeka.com. Accessed 17 Jan. 2025.
3. Rick Steves. *Rick Steves' Greece: Athens & the Peloponnese*. E-book, Avalon, 2023.
4. Steves, *Greece*.
5. "Caldera Hike with Lunch." *Santorini Walking Tours*, n.d., santoriniwalkingtours.com. Accessed 17 Jan. 2025.
6. Niki Kitsantonis. "Greece to Restrict Cruise Visits as Islands Struggle with Tourist Crowds." *New York Times*, 8 Sept. 2024, nytimes.com. Accessed 17 Jan. 2025.

CHAPTER 2. GEOGRAPHY

1. "Greece." *CIA World Factbook*, 15 Jan. 2025, cia.gov. Accessed 17 Jan. 2025.
2. "Islands." *Greek National Tourism Organisation*, n.d., visitgreece.gr. Accessed 17 Jan. 2025.
3. Loring Danforth et al. "Greece." *Britannica*, 16 Jan. 2025, britannica.com. Accessed 17 Jan. 2025.
4. "The Geography of Greece." *WorldAtlas*, n.d., worldatlas.com. Accessed 17 Jan. 2025.
5. "Crete." *Greek National Tourism Organisation*, n.d., visitgreece.gr. Accessed 17 Jan. 2025.
6. Danforth et al., "Greece."
7. "Exploring the Mountains of Greece." *Discover Greece*, n.d., discovergreece.com. Accessed 17 Jan. 2025.
8. "Pindos Mountains." *Visit Meteora*, n.d., visitmeteora.travel. Accessed 17 Jan. 2025.
9. Danforth et al., "Greece."
10. George Papadellis. "Vikos Gorge." *Shiny Greece*, 6 Mar. 2024, shinygreece.com. Accessed 17 Jan. 2025.
11. "Mt. Olympus Climb." *Explore-Share*, 5 Mar. 2020, explore-share.com. Accessed 17 Jan. 2025.
12. "Lake Trichonida." *Network of Cities with Lakes*, n.d., lakesnetwork.org. Accessed 21 Jan. 2025.
13. "Aliakmonas or Haliacmon River." *Greece Index*, n.d., greeceindex.com. Accessed 21 Jan. 2025.
14. "Greece," *CIA World Factbook*.
15. "Coastal Erosion." *Centre for Climate Adaption*, n.d., climatechangepost.com. Accessed 21 Jan. 2025.
16. "The Climate in Greece." *World Data*, Jan. 2025, worlddata.info. Accessed 21 Jan. 2025.
17. "Forests in Greece." *Greeka*, n.d., greeka.com. Accessed 21 Jan. 2025.

CHAPTER 3. PLANTS AND ANIMALS

1. "Greece—Wildlife and Biodiversity." *Working Abroad*, n.d., workingabroad.com. Accessed 21 Jan. 2025.
2. "Fifth National Report of Greece." *Convention on Biological Diversity*, 18 Mar. 2016, cbd.int. Accessed 21 Jan. 2025.
3. "ACT Campus Flora: Wild Flowers." *American College of Thessaloniki*, 20 May 2022, act.edu. Accessed 21 Jan. 2025.
4. "Wild Orchids of Greece." *Trip in Adventures*, n.d., tripin.gr. Accessed 21 Jan. 2025.
5. "Kri-Kri, the Cretan Wild Goat." *Discover Crete*, n.d., discovercrete.com. Accessed 21 Jan. 2025.
6. "Kri-Kri." *Animalia*, n.d., animalia.bio. Accessed 21 Jan. 2025.
7. "Marine Mammals of Greece." *Thalassapedia*, n.d., thalassapedia.gr. Accessed 21 Jan. 2025.
8. "Marine Mammals of Greece."

9. “Nose-Horned Viper.” *Animalia*, n.d., animalia.bio. Accessed 21 Jan. 2025.
10. “Fauna in Greece.” *Greeka*, n.d., greeka.com. Accessed 21 Jan. 2025.
11. “Birds of Greece.” *Animal Spot*, n.d., animalspot.net. Accessed 21 Jan. 2025.
12. “Walking in the Northern Pindus National Park.” *Climb Europe*, n.d., climb-europe.com. Accessed 21 Jan. 2025.
13. Joseph Florentin. “Hiking to the Peak of Smolikas Mountain.” *Planet Greece*, 29 May 2024, theplanetgreece.com. Accessed 19 Feb. 2025.
14. Charikleia Minotou. “*Caretta caretta* Turtle.” *World Wildlife Fund*, n.d., wwf.gr. Accessed 25 Jan. 2025.
15. Evan Bourtis. “Greece Conservationists Collaborate to Protect Endemic Species in Face of Climate Change.” *Mongabay*, 8 Mar. 2022, news.mongabay.com. Accessed 21 Jan. 2025.
16. Gavril Xanthopoulos et al. “Lessons Not Learned.” *International Association of Wildland Fire*, n.d., iawfonline.org. Accessed 21 Jan. 2025.

CHAPTER 4. HISTORY

1. “History of Ancient Greece.” *Greeka*, n.d., greeka.com. Accessed 21 Jan. 2025.
2. Jason Brasier. “14 Fun Facts about Greece You Never Knew You Needed.” *Real World*, 13 Nov. 2024, trafalgar.com. Accessed 21 Jan. 2025.
3. Jessica Bateman. “How Crete Changed the Course of World War Two.” *BBC*, 15 Aug. 2018, bbc.com. Accessed 21 Jan. 2025.
4. “Greek Civil War.” *Britannica*, 3 Jan. 2025, britannica.com. Accessed 21 Jan. 2025.
5. “Greece’s Debt Crisis.” *Council on Foreign Relations*, n.d., cfr.org. Accessed 21 Jan. 2025.

CHAPTER 5. PEOPLE AND CULTURE

1. “Greece.” *CIA World Factbook*, 15 Jan. 2025, cia.gov. Accessed 21 Jan. 2025.
2. “Greece.”
3. “Greece Population.” *Worldometer*, 21 Jan. 2025, worldometers.info. Accessed 21 Jan. 2025.
4. Aaron O’Neill. “Greece: The Largest Cities in 2021.” *Statista*, 12 Sept. 2024, statista.com. Accessed 21 Jan. 2025.
5. “World Religion.” *Association of Religion Data Archives*, n.d., thearda.com. Accessed 3 Feb. 2025.
6. “Religious Belief and National Belonging in Central and Eastern Europe.” *Pew Research Center*, 10 May 2017, pewresearch.org. Accessed 21 Jan. 2025.
7. “Homer.” *Lapham’s Quarterly*, n.d., laphamsquarterly.org. Accessed 21 Jan. 2025.
8. “Ten Greek Musicians of World Renown.” *Neos Kosmos*, 29 Sept. 2020, neoskosmos.com. Accessed 21 Jan. 2025.

CHAPTER 6. POLITICS

1. “Greece.” *CIA World Factbook*, 15 Jan. 2025, cia.gov. Accessed 21 Jan. 2025.
2. John S. Bowman et al. “Local Government.” *Britannica*, 20 Jan. 2025, britannica.com. Accessed 21 Jan. 2025.
3. Nektaria Stamouli. “Greece’s Conservatives Win Election Majority to Secure Second Term.” *Politico*, 26 June 2023, politico.eu. Accessed 21 Jan. 2025.
4. “Syriza.” *PolitPro*, n.d., politpro.eu. Accessed 21 Jan. 2025.
5. “PASOK.” *PolitPro*, n.d., politpro.eu. Accessed 21 Jan. 2025.
6. “Greece.”
7. “What Is NATO?” *North Atlantic Treaty Organization*, n.d., nato.int. Accessed 21 Jan. 2025.

SOURCE NOTES CONTINUED

CHAPTER 7. ECONOMICS

1. Olga Protska. "The Top 5 Most Traded Currencies in the World." *FXSSI*, 2 Mar. 2024, fxssi.com. Accessed 21 Jan. 2025.
2. "Greece." *CIA World Factbook*, 15 Jan. 2025, cia.gov. Accessed 21 Jan. 2025.
3. "Total Contribution of Travel and Tourism to GDP in Greece in 2019 and 2023, with a Forecast for 2024 and 2034." *Statista*, 26 July 2024, statista.com. Accessed 21 Jan. 2025.
4. "Share of Travel and Tourism's Total Contribution to GDP in European Union Member Countries and the United Kingdom in 2019 and 2023." *Statista*, 24 July 2024, statista.com. Accessed 25 Jan. 2021.
5. "Total Contribution of Travel and Tourism."
6. "Countries with the Highest Number of International Tourist Arrivals Worldwide from 2019 to 2023." *Statista*, 9 Jan. 2025, statista.com. Accessed 21 Jan. 2025.
7. "Greek Shipping Continues Its Run at the Top of the Tonnage Charts." *Maritime Executive*, 7 Aug. 2023, maritime-executive.com. Accessed 21 Jan. 2025.
8. "Facts and Figures." *Greece in the United States*, n.d., mfa.gr. Accessed 21 Jan. 2025.
9. "Greece," *CIA World Factbook*.
10. "Greece's Exports 2023 by Country." *Trend Economy*, n.d., trendeconomy.com. Accessed 21 Jan. 2025.
11. "Greece's Exports 2023 by Country."
12. "Greece's Exports 2023 by Country."
13. "Greece's Exports 2023 by Country."
14. "Profile of Greek Marble Quarries." *Stone Group International*, 4 Oct. 2024, stonegroup.gr. Accessed 21 Jan. 2025.
15. "Greece." *International Energy Agency*, n.d., iea.org. Accessed 21 Jan. 2025.
16. "Greece," *International Energy Agency*.
17. "Greece," *CIA World Factbook*.
18. "Greece," *International Energy Agency*.
19. "Athens Airport: Your Gateway to Meet Greece." *Athens International Airport*, n.d., athens-international-airport.com. Accessed 21 Jan. 2025.
20. "Athens Metro Network." *Greeka*, n.d., greeka.com. Accessed 21 Jan. 2025.
21. "Archaeology in Athens Metro Stations." *Archaeology Travel*, n.d., archaeology-travel.com. Accessed 21 Jan. 2025.
22. Lefteris Papadimas. "Greek Economy Surges After Decade of Pain." *Reuters*, 18 Apr. 2024, reuters.com. Accessed 21 Jan. 2025.
23. Papadimas, "Greek Economy Surges."

CHAPTER 8. GREECE TODAY

1. Stavros Koumentakis. "Family Businesses and the Economy." *Koumentakis and Associates*, 20 Sept. 2020, koumentakislaw.gr. Accessed 21 Jan. 2025.

2. "Greece." *Better Life Index*, n.d., oecdbetterlifeindex.org. Accessed 21 Jan. 2025.

3. "Greece Fact Sheet." *HIAS*, May 2024, hias.org. Accessed 21 Jan. 2025.

4. Anna Wichmann. "The Greek Diaspora around the World." *Greek Reporter*, 4 June 2024, greekreporter.com. Accessed 21 Jan. 2025.

5. Katy Fallon et al. "Greek Shipwreck: Hi-Tech Investigation Suggests Coastguard Responsible for Sinking." *Guardian*, 10 July 2023, theguardian.com. Accessed 21 Jan. 2025.

6. Aaron O'Neill. "Youth Unemployment Rate in EU Member States as of July 2024." *Statista*, 27 Sept. 2024, statista.com. Accessed 21 Jan. 2025.

INDEX

ABOUT THE **AUTHOR**

CARLA MOONEY

Carla Mooney is a graduate of the University of Pennsylvania with a degree in economics. Today, she writes for young people and is the author of many books for young adults and children. Mooney enjoys traveling to new places around the world.